Harebrained

It seemed like a good idea at the time

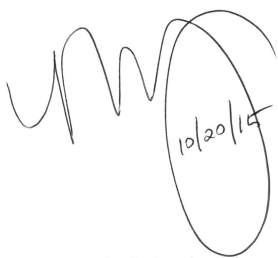

10/20/15

A collection of essays by
Meg Myers Morgan

GEM PUBLISHING

Gem Publishing ISBN:
978-0-692-41673-0

To my darling daughters.

And the man who helped me make them.

"Have some wine,"

The March Hare said in an encouraging tone.

-Lewis Carroll

Topics of Conversation

Foreword:
Humble Beginnings

Mrs. Humble was the most sought after third grade teacher in the entire elementary school, and I ran around our house screaming wildly when I discovered, over the summer, that I would be in her class.

She was a very tall and slender woman with short, tightly curled brown hair and large glasses attached to a thin, sparkly chain. She had a big smile and a loud, deep voice, and she moved about constantly with the grace of a large, leggy bird.

Her inventive classroom activities were known throughout our small, rural town; legendary were her lessons over the American political process and the supplemental activities that explored democracy. Every year, during the first week of class, students pulled slips of paper out of a hat. On each slip was the name of a famous building or monument in Washington, D.C. Each student was to create his or her building using only discarded materials.

I constructed the Lincoln Memorial using just an egg crate and watch box (I attached a picture of Lincoln onto the plastic cuff that once held a watch). Then all the students assembled the buildings into a model replica of the D.C. Mall.

This experiment always made the front page of the paper, which said more about quiet, rural living than our town's interest in democracy. But there we were, the smiling architects, proudly standing around the replica of our nation's capital for the entire town to see. Being part of her class, and that famous yearly activity, was the first time I ever felt part of something truly special.

After the fame of our accomplishment wore off, and our buildings were broken back down into trash, I felt certain someone as magical and inventive as Mrs. Humble could help me with my biggest goal in life: to write a book.

When I told her one day during free time, she pulled down her big, thick glasses, turned and twitched her head like an ostrich, and said: "Well, there's no time like the present!" And she slammed a large stack of blank paper down in front of me.

I stared at the stack, and then looked back up at her.

"Write your book." She swatted her hand toward my desk. "When you are done, you will read it to the class."

I immediately began to work.

Every day during class I'd wait for Mrs. Humble to nod at me, then I'd go to my cubby to retrieve the box that held my manuscript. Then I'd attempt to implement all the brilliant ideas I'd had since the day before when she told me it was time to stop for the day.

Mrs. Humble was clearly proud of my determination. She supported me daily. She even suggested I skip recesses until the book was complete.

And so, while my classmates all gleefully bolted for the door when the recess bell rang, I stayed alone at my desk and wrote.

When I felt satisfied with the story and happy with the illustrations, I walked my stack of construction paper to our school librarian and had her laminate every page. Then I cautiously pierced three holes on the left hand side and carefully tied each hole tightly with yellow ribbon. The book was finally complete and ready for the world.

The next day, Mrs. Humble asked me to read my book during story time.

I was nervous. But confident.

I sat in her usual spot while my classmates gathered around me. And I read aloud the book I'd spent nearly half a year composing.

When I was done, I looked around the room. My classmates seemed the same as they always did after story time—bemused and hungry—and Mrs. Humble was standing at the back of the room without so much as a smile.

"Thank you, Meg," she said.

And then we started our math lesson.

Despite the effort I put into my twelve-page book, I knew it wasn't perfect. The binding was childish. The story was too derivative (I borrowed a bit too liberally from *Beauty and the Beast*). And there was a clear overuse of blue.

The lack of quality in my product was reflected in Mrs. Humble's unsmiling face.

That day after school, I handed the book to my mother and told her she could have it. I never looked at it again.

Two important lessons came out of that experience: The first was that it is incredibly arduous to write a quality book filled with interesting and original thoughts.

And the second is that it is truly difficult to satisfy the reader.

Perhaps impossible.

Enjoy.

Table for Four

There is a charming little sandwich shop I frequent not far from our home. It's nestled in the middle of a densely populated area in a prime location in the center of one of the town's most popular shopping destinations. The beloved restaurant is known for its delectable sandwiches, creative desserts and over-priced soup.

And the shop is miniscule. Almost microscopic. Perhaps ten tiny tables in the entire storefront. As a regular, I have had plenty of opportunities to study the length of time I've had to wait for one of the tables, or for take-out, and rarely is it longer than ten minutes.

The flow of patrons never gets much more than the establishment can support.

On my drive to work every morning, I take a long, winding road to campus. I choose this road for two main reasons. One, it is the width of a four-lane road, but it is just one lane in either direction. And two, it is practically deserted.

What I can't understand is how this road, smack in the middle of the city's congestion, can be both inefficiently wide and habitually underused.

The flow of traffic never gets more than the street can support.

There are exactly two times a day when my own flow of things is almost more than I can support: 7 a.m. and 6 p.m.

At 7 a.m. I awaken our beautiful, angelic children while my husband is in the shower. First, I go to Lowery, who, immediately upon waking, begins her litany of questions including, but not limited to: "Is this a school day?" "Can I wear my cowgirl boots?" "When's Christmas?" "Is sister awake?" "Why are you wearing a robe?" "Have you not brushed your hair?" "Why are you squinting?" And on and on as I shuffle around her room trying to find her a cute shirt, clean underwear and a pair of 3T jeans without holes.

Her questions continue as we go into London's room to find the baby is awake and smiling, but with the fire of a thousand flames of hunger burning just below the surface. I spend a few minutes regulating the strength and pressure of Lowery's hug to her younger sister, and then rifle through the dresser to find a clean onesie and a pair of 9-month pants free of poop or vomit stains.

The three of us make our way down the stairs.

In the living room I place London in the exersaucer. She immediately begins to whimper. I run to make her bottle while Lowery complains of hunger. Despite reminding her every single morning that she eats breakfast at school, she always demands "a pre-breakfast snack."

As I go into the kitchen, the baby wailing and the three-year-old demanding, I find our pug Izzy dancing excitedly, reminding me that she, too, needs something edible shoved into her mouth.

The doling out of three breakfasts is always a bit of a blur, and I'm only ever about 80 percent sure the dog food and the formula make it to the correct recipients. But either way, within minutes, the baby, the dog and the three-year-old are cramming their faces with nutrients.

I know better than to get too comfortable with the momentary contentment. Soon, the bottle is drained, the dog bowl is empty and the string cheese wrapper is floating poetically to the ground.

Then it's time for everyone's bathroom breaks. I let the dog outside and watch her through the window to verify she both pees and poops, because if she doesn't do both, she'll do one in the kitchen while we are at work. I keep my eyes glued to her furry ass as I command my three-year-old to go pee in the potty while I simultaneously wrestle the nine-month-old with all the strength I have to change her diaper.

Sometimes, while monitoring, wiping or encouraging the urination and defecation of three tiny, demanding females, I begin to question my life's choices.

But somehow, the pug always manages to wind herself in circles in the back yard right around the time I hear my three-year-old flush the toilet and I toss a massively full diaper in the trash.

Then it's time to get dressed. Lowery loves to do everything all by herself, which actually means she demands I watch and praise her abilities to put underwear on correctly and button her own sweater. I love the idea of encouraging her, letting her figure things out on her own and developing her independence, but dammit sometimes I wish I had dressed her in the middle of the night while she slept so I could avoid the slow and painful process of watching my child try to work a zipper.

Instead, I pause with forced patience and remind her: "Tags in back, buttons in front."

Patiently helping Lowery get dressed is nothing compared to stuffing a nine-month-old into a onesie. Or a shirt. Or pants. Somewhere, in the midst of trying to force my sweet baby's doughy legs into a pair of stretchy leggings, I lose my will to parent.

Once the girls are dressed—the dog stays naked—I put the baby on the floor so I can style the three-year-old's hair. In theory, I enjoy fixing her hair immensely.

In practice, there are a lot of tears.

For the past year I've tried many products to help with her tangles, and searched high and low for a specialty comb with teeth set apart so wide it's really just a BBQ fork.

Each day I believe we are closer and closer to scream-free combing, but that's just called optimism, and optimism can't get you as far in life as Johnson & Johnson detangler.

After the girls have been fed, emptied, dressed and combed, it's time for socks and shoes. Lowery cares immensely about what shoes she wears, which I've decided to find endearing. While she runs around looking for her desired pair, I run around looking for all of Lowery's baby dolls, because on their little plastic feet are layers and layers of London's socks. If I find a pair of matching baby socks, I remind myself to buy a lottery ticket on the way to work, but in general, the baby goes to school with mismatched socks, or, if needed, a small mitten on each foot.

My husband comes down the stairs as the girls are by the front door ready for him to take them to day care. As they walk out the front door, my three-year-old's curls bouncing as she skips, and my youngest smiling at me from my husband's arms, I immediately ache for them to be near me again.

But before I allow the feeling of unconditional love to take over, I slam the door, and lock it. Coffee must be made.

After some caffeine and a warm breakfast, I feel more regulated and can calmly get myself ready for the day. I enjoy my drive to work. Just a short ten minutes from my house to campus down the wide, quiet, curvy street where I drive past the quaint little sandwich shop as I mentally prepare for the day ahead.

In my general day-to-day work I engage in a number of personality-intensive activities, like back-to-back meetings with students, making presentations out in the community, or teaching a three-hour class. There are rarely moments of quietly sitting and thinking in my office, and not just because I have no interest in doing that, but because my position is one in which interacting with students, administrators and community leaders is expected.

This works well because I get all my energy from others. I tend to drain it from them and leave them for dead. And while I fully recognize I'm in a good job that plays to my strengths, at the end of the day I still find myself feeling as though it is all a bit more energy than my body can support.

Especially knowing I'm heading home for the 6 o'clock hour.

I spend the ten-minute drive home, down the wide, curvy, quiet street, past the adorable little sandwich shop, trying to regulate my flow of thoughts and energy. And to prepare for the upcoming flurry of chaos I'm about to endure.

There is a moment in every person's life that defines his or her character. Mine is the moment I put the key in the door upon returning home.

In my arms is my nine-month-old, and beside me is my energetic three-year-old continuing on with her litany of questions that include, but are not limited to: "What's for dinner?" "You know I love macaroni, right?" "Are we having macaroni for dinner?" "Mom, what's your favorite dinner?" "Is it macaroni?" "Is Izzy awake?" "Where's dad?" "Did you go to work today?" "Are you going to make macaroni?"

She rattles on as I fiddle with the key, the baby grunting and clapping because she's aware food awaits on the other side of the door.

Once the door is open, Lowery bursts into the house, running around wildly while stripping her clothes off piece by piece. I'm relieved to see my husband is pulling into the drive.

He comes in and instructs Lowery to pick up her coat, gloves, hat and that day's artwork as he walks to the kitchen to prepare London her dinner. As he wipes down the high chair and mixes up oatmeal, I send Izzy outside.

While standing at the window, staring at pug butt, I yell at Lowery to stop running around topless and go to the bathroom. She politely tells me that that is of no interest to her. This escalates quickly into the kind of yelling match my three-year-old and I have perfected.

It ends with her finally relenting just as the pug leaves a pile on the porch.

My husband, having prepared the meal for the baby, comes to my side to help hold her down while I attempt to change her diaper.

There's a rash.

I dab a bit of ointment on it, but she sticks her hand into it and tries to bring it to her mouth. My husband grabs each hand, and I pull wipe upon wipe out of the container, unable to regulate their flow. But no matter how much I try, the ointment keeps spreading all over the baby, the table and, somehow, my elbow.

As the medicine mangle continues, my husband and I communicate through huffs and puffs. Izzy begins scratching feverishly at the back door, the baby wails in frustration, and my three-year-old tugs gently at my pant leg.

Covered in diaper rash cream and fighting a baby who possesses inexplicable upper body strength, I turn my head to see Lowery's bright, happy face, surrounded by white ringlets, as she asks:

"Can I have some macaroni?"

At some point, within minutes, the chaos dies down, and Jim and I are able to enjoy the giggles of our children. We are able to eat dinner and talk to one another and revel in the beauty and wonder of the little life we've created. And eventually, darkness falls and slumber awaits us.

As I lie in bed, waiting for sleep to take over, I enumerate the struggles that await me when I wake. How will I manage the rush of 7 a.m.? Wait, do I have clean socks for the girls? How will I deal with the day at work? Crap, where did I put those lecture notes? How will I get through the 6 o'clock hustle? Do I have anything in the fridge for dinner?

The only way I can regulate my worry is to think of my drive to and from work. Down the wide, curvy street and past the little sandwich shop.

Where every table is full but the line is not too long.

Carried Away

For a brief period in my life, I was a mascot. A kangaroo, actually.

Carey the Caring Kangaroo.

My first job out of college was with a very well-known and respected nonprofit organization. In the 70s, the organization developed Carey the Kangaroo as part of a program to teach children about kindness. Or reading. Or maybe it was hygiene. The details are a bit fuzzy, but during my first week on the job I found the costume stuffed in a closet and begged to put it on.

A star was born.

The costume was large and bulky, with over dramatized hips and a thick heavy tail that swung to the beat of my gait. The belly was full of what I can only describe as dirty mattress foam, and the material down the arms was akin to the hair of a mangy Newfoundland.

The gloves were enormous and only had four fingers, which meant keeping them on while waving to adoring crowds was difficult. To counter this, I developed a distinctive Carey wave in which I stretched my arms out in front of me, parallel to the ground, and held my hands straight up with the palms out, as though I was trying to get everyone to stop in the name of love. And with rapid and quick spasms, I'd shake my hands as though I was waxing on and waxing off.

The feet were the size and shape of clown feet, with three furry, hard balls making up the toes. Each foot slipped over my normal street shoes. But the foot bed was made of thick, inflexible plastic, which made walking with a normal heel-to-toe step impossible. So I had to lift my entire leg up high, creating a 90-degree angle, with every step.

This is why Godzilla walked the way he did.

The hood of the costume was large, and the mouth served as the windshield. But my vision was impaired because Carey didn't have a particularly toothy grin. The nose aligned with the top of my head, and was hollowed out. I mounted a hand-held, battery-operated fan inside the nose with a wad of Velcro. The rest of the head, and the bendable floppy ears, reached out and above me, allowing Carey to stand more than six and a half feet tall.

I'm 5'3".

There was a lot I never imagined before becoming a mascot. For starters, kids were trickier than I thought they'd be. Too young and they were scared of me, too old and they found me annoying.

Or that I would always smile for pictures.

I had beer cans thrown at me. I had my tail pulled. I had my belly punched. And once, a drunk college guy dry humped me for a laugh.

Hockey fans. Am I right?

Being a mascot was a culture. Or, to be more precise, a sub-culture. An underground world of people who could manipulate a cumbersome body with limited mobility and make it look easy. A group committed to letting the world delight in the splendor of a charismatic creature who was silently difficult to bring to life.

The best moment was after an event, back in the locker room, or behind a stadium, or in a trailer, where it was safe to take off the mascot hood. There was always someone to hand me a cold drink. Sometimes a beer, if it was a baseball game. But often just an ice-cold water that always felt so good after climbing out of the 20-pound furry suit in the hot Oklahoma summer.

The drink was worth the thirst.

Most weekends I had an event. I was either throwing the first pitch at a minor-league baseball game, dropping the puck at a hockey game, tossing the coin at a college football game, attending a ribbon cutting, Oktoberfest, local television appearances or charity events.

I even did a fundraising walk for some incurable disease in which a guide had to accompany me so I wouldn't wander off the trail.

But the most challenging mascot event I attended was the community's annual Mascot Dodgeball Tournament, in which all area mascots participated during halftime of an arena football game.

When I arrived at the arena, a skinny guy wearing a headset took me down to the locker room. There I was given a seat among my co-competitors, which included: the Bookworm from the downtown library. A Cup from Quiznos. An Otter from the local water park. A Bull from the minor league baseball team, a Trojan from an area high school and numerous others who sat in the locker room, hoods off, politely making small talk before we had to fight to the death.

Unbeknownst to any of us, we were to be introduced much like a football player—over the loud speaker—and then we were to run full speed across the length of the football field in our cumbersome, hot, vision-impairing suits.

I made it about 20 yards before I stopped, breathing heavily, thought fuck it, and walked the rest of the way.

The game was clearly rigged so that the opposite team would win. The way to rig a mascot dodgeball game is to put the vision and dexterity impaired against those who, say, didn't wear mascot hoods or gloves. Therefore, the Trojan, who was just a buff junior wearing chest armor, was free to run about and mercilessly pelt the fully cloaked.

Luckily, the ample padding around the ass and hips meant I was protected from any real bodily harm. But it also meant I couldn't feel when I had been hit with a ball, and therefore eliminated. The referee had to run to me, tap me on the shoulder and yell into the kangaroo's mouth that I had been hit in the knee by the Chick-Fil-A Cow.

And yet, he kept yelling excitedly, I was the last mascot standing on the losing team.

Even in a loss there is victory.

The summer before my junior year of high school, I underwent total hip replacement surgery to correct for injuries sustained in a car accident while vacationing with my family in New Mexico when I was eight years old.

Hip replacement surgery is typically performed on the elderly. My grandmother had one when she was 80 after falling in the bathroom. But it's not completely unheard of for infants with hip dysplasia to have this in their first year of life. Children with juvenile arthritis or pediatric cancer sometimes need one. But in general, it's rare to replace a joint on a teenager.

As a result of the car accident, I broke my right femur and was in a chest-to-toe body cast for most of the fourth grade. But when the cast came off, it became clear that damage had also been done to my left hip. The impact on my body—having been thrown free of the car and landing in a ditch—actually destroyed the hip joint, which began losing circulation and, essentially, shriveling up like a rotting piece of fruit. This meant that from the age of eight until the hip replacement surgery when I was 15, I walked with a very severe limp.

My junior high years need no explanation.

Much of my formative years seemed to have taken place inside doctors' waiting rooms. Surgeon after surgeon turned me away because they either couldn't determine what was best for my hip joint at such a young age, or they were unwilling to perform the only surgery that could stop the pain and correct the limp.

My parents tirelessly researched surgery options and surgeons, even flying me to other states to meet with specialists. After seven years of consultations, research and physical assessments, we found a highly respected specialist who was willing to take my case.

At the time, even seven years after the accident, I was still too traumatized to even talk about the wreck. Or my injuries. While my classmates certainly noticed my limp, I never mentioned it. And I did everything in my power to distract from its obviousness.

I mostly just sat around. And developed a personality.

Leading up to the surgery I had to regularly give blood to build up a supply in the event I needed a transfusion during the procedure. I continually received "Most Valuable and Selfless Donor" cards from the blood bank, even though no one—except possibly me—would ever benefit from my donations.

I was pulled out of school constantly for numerous pre-op appointments. The last one—during which I had to give a urine sample—was during my first real period. And therefore, my transition into womanhood was captured for posterity in a small, plastic, sterilized cup.

The day of the surgery, I felt pretty fearless. I didn't think the surgery would make my pain *more* severe or my limp *more* noticeable. So it was pretty effortless to lie back, inhale the gas and wait for everything to be corrected.

And when I woke up, everything nearly was.

The sensation was surreal. It's the same sensation you feel when you've been in a concert for hours and walk out into the quiet night.

Back then, patients were required to stay completely off their operated side for six weeks. So I spent the summer in my father's lumpy recliner reading. My parents hustled in and out for work, while I spent the majority of my days reading or watching movies they would start when they were in to check on me. Surgery is limiting, sure, but not as much as VHS tapes were.

They rented a freestanding potty chair, which was, essentially, a large plastic basin with legs. It stood beside my recliner. I would pull myself up by gripping the doorframe, then pivot on my good leg, lower myself down, and shit in the bucket.

Character building at its finest.

Even though the surgeon didn't typically recommend physical therapy after a hip replacement due to the age of most patients, my parents hired a therapist knowing that walking without a limp was paramount. It would require a full summer of rigorous, physical work.

Denise, a physical therapist and a long-time family friend, came to our house twice a week. Before we began our sessions, she would always spend time just chatting with me. I think on some level she understood that a girl going through puberty, while forced to sit in a recliner next to a bucket full of her own shit, just needed to talk.

Each week she'd give me a small, obtainable goal. Like standing with a walker and lifting my operated leg out to the side for ten reps. When I had built up to that, she'd have me practice getting in and out of a chair without the cane. Later we worked on balance. And finally, one day, she told me I would be putting half my weight on my operated side.

My parents came home from work to watch.

I stood in the dining room holding on to the walker, all my weight on my good side. I white-knuckled the walker as I slowly allowed my body to shift off of the right side. And I finally put my foot down.

A few weeks later she had her final task for me. She brought me an ice-cold cherry limeade on a hot, July day. But she left it outside.

I was told I could have it, but I'd have to go get it myself.

And one tiny, timid step at a time, I got up out of the recliner, walked slowly to the front door, stepped gingerly down the five steps, shuffled barefoot out into the grass and grabbed the large drink sitting on the hood of her car, the plastic lid glinting in the sun.

When she suggested we go back inside to escape the heat, I tried to hand her my drink.

"Nope," she said. "Carry it."

In retrospect, the load wasn't all that heavy.

After receiving a promotion at the nonprofit agency, I had to prioritize my new responsibilities. It was suggested I transfer Carey the Kangaroo to an intern or a high school volunteer.

From there, Carey bounced around from interns to new hires and even a few random employees who just wanted to see what it was like to bring the creature to life.

And every time I helped a newcomer into the suit, I demonstrated how to tuck in the mattress material so it wouldn't rub any skin and would inflate the pouch to an adorable degree. I'd explain how to turn on the nose fan. How to do the Carey wave to keep the gloves from falling off. The Godzilla walk to prevent tripping.

Most everyone was surprised at how heavy and hot the suit was. Shocked at how little they could see. Frustrated by how difficult it was to move about. And nearly every single inhabitant would want to know what to do if they started to get hot or dizzy or just tired of wearing the suit before an event was over.

The truth was, this was bound to happen. The body was heavy, limiting and cumbersome. So when they asked for my advice on how to sustain the effort through an entire two-hour event out in the hot Oklahoma sun, I'd just shrug. I'd remind them that there would be an icy cold beverage waiting at the end.

And then I'd stand on my tiptoes and yell into the kangaroo's mouth the only thing they could do until then:

Carry on.

Portuguese Man-of-War

The most rigorous class I took in college was a journalism course with an older, slightly bitter lady who once managed the crime beat for some newspaper in LA.

At the beginning of class each week she would hand us a slip of paper as we walked into the room. On that paper would be a prompt, typically just a few sentences. We would get exactly ten minutes to write a full news story based on the prompt. When time was up, she would clap her hands sharply and randomly point at a student to read his or her work.

Rarely would anyone get through a paragraph, let alone finish an entire article, before she would sharply clap again and say, "You buried the lead! Next!" Or, "I'm not hooked! Next!" And on and on, slapping her papers on someone's keyboard or flicking her hand in dismissal.

One day my prompt said something like this: *Mayor of Florida town warning citizens and tourists about an unprecedented number of Portuguese Men-of-War on the shoreline. They are prone to attack and their poison can cause serious harm. Alert authorities if you spot one, and step cautiously around them.*

Thrilled by the day's prompt, I set to work, certain this was going to be my most dramatic and impressive piece yet. At the ten-minute mark, she pointed to the student beside me as the first to read.

I was surprised to hear his article and its passive attitude toward these vengeful men ready to attack any American who set foot on the beach. When he talked about the importance of being able to recognize a Portuguese Man-of-War, I chuckled to myself, thinking that their poisonous spears and face paint would be a dead give-away. And when he explained how they "shimmy" out of the water, I stopped and thought maybe that was just how the Europeans train their men to fight. Shake the shoulders back and forth to the beat of government-issued steel drums while walking toward the enemy; it lures them into a false sense of security.

The next student called on to read her article had written rhapsodically about their beauty. The closest I'd come to seeing one was the Spaniard in my advanced Calc class, but I assumed anyone from that region has the same lovely skin tone. When she talked about seeing some off the coast of Hawaii, I wondered why everyone was so concerned about the Middle East. Seemed we had bigger problems in Portugal. And only when she mentioned getting to feed one at an aquarium in Cleveland did I start to get a tad suspicious that maybe I didn't have a fucking clue what was going on.

This was far from my first, or last, bout of indefensible confusion.

Tone Deaf

One time, while driving to the movies with my husband, the song "Money for Nothing" by Dire Straits came on. When I heard the chorus I laughed, which confused Jim. I explained that this song always struck me as funny because most banks offer free checking, so why make such a big deal about it?

Silence.

A few minutes later Jim said, "You know it's 'money for nothing and your *chicks* for free,' right?"

Word Confusion

Only recently did I discover that "Aison" isn't a word. As in the classically boring John Malkovich film, *Dangerously Aisons.*

South Paw

I do not know my right from my left. Laugh all you want. Feel free to give me lots of helpful tips to remember the difference. I know, I know, my left finger and thumb make an L.

You don't get it.

I truly do not know them. I assume for others it is a reflex that is as natural as "touch your nose" or "look up." But I have to stop for a few moments and think it through.

It's understandable. I'm left handed. Many lefties who grew up with right-handed learning instruments (like scissors, school desks, siblings) struggle to understand direction, and some (it's an embarrassingly small number) have trouble distinguishing their left from their right. During Driver's Ed my teacher almost shit himself when he said, "Turn left" into what would have been a church parking lot, and I instead tried to turn right. Into a ditch.

Feeling frustrated by my inability to master something so simple, my father attempted to console me by saying he had read somewhere that Da Vinci (also left handed) didn't know his left from his right either and that he could only distinguish between the two when he picked up a paint brush. He explained that numerous people with extremely high IQs have struggled with their left and right, even Einstein.

And there's nothing smarter than rationalizing away stupidity by claiming it's extreme intellect.

Facial Tics

I cannot read digital clocks. Yes, *digital.* When I see the numbers on a digital clock, 11:32, I understand that it is eleven thirty two; I'm not such a dumbass I can't read *numbers.* I just can't read *time* in numbers. I need to see numbers in a pie-like perspective so that I know how many pieces of pie I have until my next appointment, or how many pieces of pie I have been waiting in line.

Phonics

I was surprised to learn, a few years back, that the silent game in which you act out a person, place or thing in order to have your teammate guess is spelled with a "CH." It is not, as I had assumed, Shhhhrades.

Holy Optical Illusion, Batman!

I always thought bats had rounded teeth because the Batman symbol, which shows the open mouth of a bat, features curved molars.

Positively Negative

My sister enjoys teasing me about the time she tutored me in Algebra. Keep in mind that my sister is a mechanical engineer and I am, well, creative with colored pencils.

She got frustrated at my inability to grasp the concept of negative numbers. I thought then, and still strongly believe, that a negative sign and a minus sign are two different symbols with very different functions. So, to me, 5 - 2 cannot produce the same result as 5 + -2. You see, in our sixth grade Algebra book the "-" sign was always just slightly (perhaps a millimeter) longer when it was used for minus than when it was used to denote negative. My sister tugged violently at her hair, reminding me that minus and negative are the same damn thing, but the book depicted them differently.

And while I'm never going to see them as the same function, I later wondered if it was somewhat impressive that I even noticed the infinitesimal difference between the signs in the book. Perhaps that, in and of itself, meant I was a genius.

My sister would tell you that's a negative.

Die Hard

In the sixth grade, when I first made the switch from glasses to contacts, I struggled to remember to take them out at night. I'd wake up each morning thinking I was cured.

My eye doctor reprimanded me constantly. And though he protested my lazy eye care, I never changed my ways. To help, he switched me from regular contacts to the daily disposable kind when I went off to college. At the end of every night it was truly exhilarating to just pull them out of my eyes and throw them in the trash. No contact solution. No unscrewing the tiny cap on the contact case. No cleaning.

Just extract and toss.

But because taking my contacts out was the last thing I did before bed, I often just threw them in the toilet, which was closer to the sink. Whereas the trash can was clear on the other side of the toilet, adding another step to my nightly routine.

This plan worked beautifully until my roommate started acting strangely. All of a sudden she seemed annoyed with me. Wouldn't even make eye contact. Finally, after weeks of the cold shoulder, I sat her down and asked what was wrong. She explained that I was a pain in her ass.

Literally.

Apparently, when contacts are left out in the air, they shrivel and become extremely hard, resembling a small and wrinkled shard of glass. And apparently, once my contacts were out, and my vision was impaired, my aim wasn't great. So, when I threw my contacts into the toilet, they landed on the seat. Thus leaving two shriveled, invisible shards of glass for my roommate to sit on the next morning.

After my laughter subsided, I promised her that I would never throw my contacts in—or at—the toilet again. I would take the extra step and throw them in the trash can.

Cold turkey.

And I kept my promise through graduation. But then I moved away, to a new town and into an apartment where I would live alone for the first time.

Without the pressure of a roommate's judgment, I, once again, became lax in my nightly routine. I would lay in bed reading until my eyes burned. Instead of making the effort to get up and throw my contacts in the trash, I often just took them out and laid them on the nightstand. The next morning, after they had dried into glass splinters, I would scoop them up and throw them away.

When I got married and was again living with another person, I found the rigor of my nightly ritual loosening even further. Perhaps unconditional love made me lazy. I lapsed into an even worse behavior: leaving the dried glass shards on the nightstand and not throwing them out in the morning.

After a while, the pile of contacts would become so large they would fall off the nightstand. And in so doing, they would imbed themselves in the carpet. And sometimes I would awaken to the whimper of my husband, who had stepped on a rogue shard. But he was too kind to mention how my bad habit was hurting him. He refused to believe I had any flaws.

When we sold our house, after living there six years together, and were packing up to move to our new home, Jim and I would call out "New House Rules." Once, while I was running around the house looking for a light bulb, I yelled to him outside, "New House Rule: Keep all light bulbs in a central location!" Once when it was raining hard and Jim was trying to leave for work he yelled, "New House Rule: Don't leave umbrellas in the car!" And on and on. "New House Rule: Run the dishwasher every night!" "New House Rule: Hang up our coats when we come in the door!" A verbal promise of the different ways we would live in our new home.

Cleaner, nicer, better.

The night before the movers came, Jim was in our bedroom moving furniture away from the wall. I was in the bathroom packing toiletries when I heard him yell, "New House Rule!" I paused to listen for him to announce the new rule, but there was silence. I walked into our bedroom to see him pointing at the spot where my nightstand had been. I looked down to see a pile, perhaps six inches tall and a foot wide. It was six years of dried contacts.

Or as some experts call it, rock bottom.

When the movers came and took all the boxes from our home, all the furniture from the rooms and all the artwork from the walls, I felt a sense of relief. I put the extender on the vacuum and in one quick motion, with the sound of glass tinkling up the tube, I undid all the damage I had done the past half decade. I was giving myself a clean start. I handed the vacuum to the movers and walked outside to see how my husband was doing with packing the garage.

If my bad habit of extreme laziness made a cubic foot of mess, my husband's bad habit of intense organization led to a 400-square-foot mess. Stacks and stacks of paperwork, neatly organized in boxes, drawers and fireproof tubs.

Every cancelled check since the first one he ever wrote. Every bill he'd ever received, grouped by vendor and alphabetized. Every major newspaper's coverage of the OKC bombing, 9/11, Katrina and the 2008 presidential election. I'd been in the garage many, many times over the years, but mostly we used it for storage. So I had never really *looked*.

I suppose I always knew my husband had a problem. If you can call it a problem. He's meticulous. Precise. Never loses his car keys or forgets a doctor's appointment. And the way he keeps our checkbook makes me hope for an audit just to render the IRS agents speechless when they see his bookkeeping.

But I didn't know we had let the back of the nightstand, or the inside of the garage, get so bad.

It'd be easy to call Jim a hoarder. But if I called *TLC,* I know the camera crew would show up, take one look at the garage and its extreme order—and the *lack* of cat poop and empty egg shells—and walk away telling their producer there's no story here. But with the movers impatiently waiting for us to pack up the remains of the garage, I looked around and wondered if Jim was, in fact, a hoarder.

The slips of paper he saved about his health insurance from his first job. His orientation packet from USC film school. Every *Star Wars* trading card (three sets of each one, he explained; one to play with and two to keep in mint condition for resale).

And magazines. Oh, the magazines.

But as I looked, really looked at what he had saved, robust a collection as it was, I could see he had made choices. He didn't actually keep *everything*. He kept things that meant something. When I found the first note I ever wrote him, just a random piece of paper with directions to a restaurant scribbled on it, I realized my husband wasn't a hoarder. He was sentimental.

And while I was furious at the amount we had to sift through that day, I didn't want him to change. I didn't want there to be a New House Rule in which Jim was forced to throw away things that mattered.

But that wasn't how Jim saw it. He was angry with himself for weeks. After we were officially moved into the new house and rid of our old one, he spent his nights and weekends out in the garage going through all his collections. He recycled bins and bins of papers and newspapers and receipts and notes. He donated books and magazines. I would peek out the window to see him shredding documents and cursing himself by the light of the moon. I felt conflicted because, while I was loving how little clutter we had, I worried he would throw away too much. Even stuff we really should keep.

Changing environments or life circumstances can modify behavior. My father-in-law quit smoking the day my husband was born. I stopped biting my nails when I got my first job out of college. Lowery gave up the bottle at 11 months when she discovered how she could shove avocado in her mouth by herself. And Jim stopped hoarding his life away once he really started living it.

In the new house I find that, so far, I have done a load of laundry and a load of dishes every night. I keep our jackets hung up and towels off the bathroom floor. We cook more, walk more and rest more. Not because the new house is magical, or perfect, or even that much better than our old house. It's just that the move gave us a chance to reevaluate our behaviors. An excuse to change.

But there's a difference between a habit and a personality.

After a month of living in the new house, I was tidying up the living room and noticed some paper stuck between two books on the shelf. It was a piece of junk mail addressed to Jim and me, or "current resident." I wondered why Jim had stuck this in the books.

Figuring out why didn't take long. It was the first piece of mail we received at our new home. And he stuck it between two books thinking this was different from stacking it neatly in the garage.

It was a new way of doing an old habit.

I tucked it back between the books and went about my business. I decided not to nag him about I had found. Mostly because this morning, I awoke to a very familiar sound:

The harrowing bellow of a person with glass in his ass.

Waxing Poetic

The amount of time women must spend in awkward positions at the mercy of other women, just for aesthetics and relaxation, is mind-boggling. Head full of foil in front of the hair stylist. Lying naked in front of the masseuse. Feet in the hands of a kneeling pedicurist. Facing the facialist without makeup. And, like today, spread eagle wearing a paper thong in front of the esthetician holding a tongue depressor covered in boiling hot wax.

Yes. I had my very first bikini wax.

And I was an absolute champ.

I'd always contemplated doing it. And by always, I mean every time I shave. Or swim. Or see a Groupon for half off. Price, that is. But intentions are just that until you see a sandwich board outside a dark basement salon advertising a bikini wax for "Cheap! Cheap! Cheap!" That, coupled with my upcoming 30th birthday trip to Vegas, led me to finally drop my drawers.

When I called to set up the appointment, I immediately confessed to the receptionist that it was my first time to get a bikini wax. When she didn't seem all that thrown or surprised by this, I still felt the need to further explain that I am a mother and have been really busy with graduate school the last couple of years, and you know, the recession.

A few more details of my life and a couple more excuses about my lack of maintenance, and even eventually throwing out, "Just 'cause I've never hired a gardener doesn't mean I don't trim the bushes," led to silence on her end. A few moments later she said, "M'am, is four o'clock this afternoon okay with you?"

When I arrived at the salon wearing my most presentable pair of underwear, all of the staff members were in the lobby enjoying coffee. As I walked in, I felt all eyes on me. It was clear I was the only client in the building, so they all had to know I was Hairy McTalksalot here for her wash and wax.

I was led back to a room where there was what looked like a card table covered by a towel next to a crock-pot full of melted candles.

"So, what kind of waxing were you interested in today?" the waxer asked as she handed me a pair of disposable underwear.

"Um. I'm not sure," I replied. "Topiary?"

"No. I meant, bikini or Brazilian?" she clarified.

"Oh. Bikini," I muttered. "But more like one with the skirt bottom."

I was surprised at her ease in the situation. She pulled my dress up to see what kind of work was ahead of her. She looked at the area long enough to let me know she was strategizing, but not so long that I started to feel bad for my husband.

The experience wasn't too unlike giving birth. I was spread eagle with searing pain in my groin while the professional in the room just looked at my area with the eye of an expert, unabashedly gazing at something so personal in such a clinical way.

"You know," she said between pulls. "I've seen everything."

"My OBGYN says the same thing. But that never makes me feel better."

But, just like during childbirth, about halfway through I began not to care. I relaxed into the frogger position and tried not to look at what was on the strips of paper she pulled back.

"Tell me your craziest story," I asked while she was in a particularly delicate place.

"Oh, let's see," she said, pausing and holding up a dripping spatula of wax. "Well, I can either tell you about the 60-year-old female who had never shaved once in her life. Or the man with the hairy penis."

"I'm gonna need to hear both," I said, wondering if there was any chance I'd be one of the freak shows she'd talk about to her next client.

But she worked quickly, talking in between the sounds of heavy duty Velcro being released, and assuring me in a subtle way that everything she was looking at was run-of-the-mill.

There was one particularly awkward moment: the clean up. This involved using a substance that would remove all the left over wax from the area. And while this sounded like an easy enough endeavor, it turned out to be a bit intrusive. But she assured me that if she didn't do this thoroughly my ass cheeks might get seared together.

All in a day.

Truthfully, the experience made me proud to be a woman. I mean, pissed that vaginas need such upkeep, but proud to be part of the gender. Because what other gender can stomach such experiences? Getting a bikini wax is right up there with getting a pap smear or having an episiotomy. But that's the thing about vaginas: they can handle it. Especially if there's another woman in the room rooting for you.

Now I feel ready for our upcoming trip. Actually, I feel ready for the world. After letting a stranger scorch my nether regions with lava hot goo, I truly feel like there is nothing I can't do.

But for now I'll go to Vegas and sit by the pool with my husband.

Happily enjoying the breeze.

Photogenic

My dad responds the same way whenever anyone says he is photogenic: he says he must not be very attractive in actuality, and that the person's surprise at him looking good in a photograph somewhat corroborates this.

A few weeks back a friend was at our house looking at a family photo I have framed on our wall. "Meg, you are so photogenic!" she declared. And my dad was right—she seemed surprised I looked good in the picture.

That I'm photogenic is the most common compliment I receive. I can count on a few fingers the times anyone has told me, in person, that I was beautiful. I may not give good face, but I take a damn fine photo.

A good picture can really boost my self-esteem. It almost undoes the damage done by catching a glimpse of myself in the mirror when stepping out of the shower. But these kind of elevating images come few and far between.

Given the digital capabilities, smart phones and the world of social media, taking an abundance of pictures is standard. Manipulating them with filters that brighten the skin, or enhance the colors, is easy. And storing them in cheap, readily available memory is encouraged. In the modern world there is no excuse for not constantly documenting my life.

Which is why I've mostly forgiven my parents for the pathetic lack of pictures there are of me growing up.

I've seen one Polaroid in which I look to be about three years old and another from my high school graduation. In the middle are a few of me at home with my siblings and at camp with my friends. But trying to convince me I was actually raised by my parents is challenging for them.

There's simply not enough evidence.

My oldest child, however, will one day marvel at the vast collection of pictures I have of her. Thousands of pictures. All of her many expressions, outfits, milestones, trips, toys, parties, meals, doctor visits and play dates. One day she can look back and see how much her parents loved her, how much we captured, witnessed and were excited by every fucking thing she ever did.

And for a while, I felt that the beautiful pictures of my child were all I was capable of offering her. It was my only form of parenting.

When I was pregnant with Lowery, I was hell-bent on a number of parenting choices. The most fervent of these was breastfeeding.

I wouldn't say I had a desire to breastfeed. I would say I had an obsessive passion to breastfeed. I read countless books on the topic, clicked through endless websites, visited with my friends who had successfully breastfed, pitied those who were unsuccessful, and signed my husband and me up for classes in which I dunked my nipple in the mouth of a surprised-looking doll.

I talked endlessly about it to everyone. Registered for a breast pump with more horsepower than my car. I bought heaps of nursing bras, nursing tops and breast pads. I refused my friends' offers of used bottles and bought extremely stylish apron-like contraptions that would hide my baby and exposed breasts as I fed her at places like the Farmers' Market and the cloth diaper emporium.

I spoke to my doctor about making sure after delivery that my child's lips would touch my nipple as quickly as possible. Was there a way I could bend myself into a position such that I could breastfeed my child as she was coming out of me?

My labor with Lowery lasted 18 hours, with two and a half hours of pushing. When it was finally over, I was told my vagina had ripped in the shape of a Y.

Cursive or sans serif, I had wondered.

The process of stitching my typography back together took an hour and a half. Trying to breastfeed through the pain and exhaustion was a fool's errand. But I tried. My child seemed tired and annoyed, but she suckled enough to let me know that I was already mastering breastfeeding.

And motherhood.

On our second day home with her, I began to notice she was looking more jaundice with each passing hour. And though I was breastfeeding her every two hours, she hadn't had a single wet diaper.

When I noticed the whites of her eyes were the color of summer squash, we decided to call the doctor. They said to run, not walk, to the nearest emergency room.

We assumed that she just needed to sit under the Bili lights for a few hours until the jaundice subsided. But her blood work showed that my child was severely dehydrated. She would need to stay in the hospital for several days to get her fluids up. She was to be under strict observation.

The theory was that my milk had not come in and the colostrum I was producing was so minimal that my child was suffering from dehydration, or starvation. So while my three-day-old daughter was hooked up to an IV with a 5-pound bag of fluid—she looked so tiny, small and scared—I was to sit beside her and use a breast pump anytime I wasn't actually breastfeeding to encourage my milk supply.

For three days I sat, in a bathrobe, still bleeding from my sutures, having had no sleep since giving birth, with a pump on each breast, looking in shame at the bottles not filling up. I would stop pumping every hour and bring my daughter to the breast. This was difficult as her arm was so bandaged with IVs. When she would finish, I was back on the pump. I would give her whatever little I eeked out over the hour and then try to breastfeed again. She seemed to prefer my left breast, which had my tits resembling a sideways semicolon. A nipple wink.

For 72 solid hours every doctor who entered the room would barely look at me. They were there to check on my child; I wasn't their concern. Even when I began to cry with one of the pediatricians, telling him I was in so much pain and wondering if I should give up the breastfeeding to concentrate on getting rest, I was told that nursing was my only job.

It was the beginning of motherhood making me feel invisible.

And so there in the children's hospital, my week-old infant lying in a crib with tubes running in and out of her, my legs swelling, my stitches throbbing, having not showered, slept or left the 12-cubic-foot room in three days, I had what I can only describe as a mental breakdown.

And once the tears started, they didn't stop for three solid months.

It wasn't just that I had failed in delivering on the many promises I had made to myself about how I would mother. It wasn't just the brutal physical trauma I endured during childbirth. It was that, in a moment in which unconditional love should have taken over, unbridled selflessness should have surfaced, it didn't and I was unable to rise up and meet the needs of my child.

I think most mothers only know, and sign up for, about 70 percent of what parenting turns out to be. The other 30 percent we don't know about until it's too late, and at that point it seems selfish to complain. Postpartum depression, for me, was dealing with that 30 percent. Namely the part in which I felt myself disappear. Slip away. Fall apart.

Part of this was due to how I was treated, and pressured, during my child's first days of life. But a big part was on me. At any point I could have looked at my breasts not inflating and switched to formula. I could have handed my child to my husband or my mother and gone and taken a nap. I could have been much more open about how depressed and scared I felt. And I could have admitted that I didn't feel bonded to my sweet, beautiful baby.

Eventually, I did all of those things. And when I finally did, nearly everything in my life, and in the life of my child, instantly improved.

But it took as long as it did because I was terrified of what it meant about me as a woman. What it said about me as a mother. Society is not terribly kind to women. It's even worse to mamas.

The 72 hours on the breast pump had me convinced that the best thing for my child was the one thing I couldn't do. And the parade of doctors had me convinced that my health, my wellbeing, my sanity were no longer of concern. I only existed to be a mother.

And I couldn't even do that.

But eventually, with the help of my husband and some friends, and a random stranger in Starbucks—who looked at my sad face carrying my one-month-old child and said, "I promise it gets better"—I switched to formula, I took some naps, I sought medical care for the depression, and I cut myself some slack.

Because I wasn't able to do the one maternal thing I was most excited about—breastfeeding—I tried to focus on things I was good at.

Like how I tell my students when they take final exams: start with the easiest questions to build up confidence.

So I started taking pictures. The proof of life.

And it helped.

It encouraged me to get dressed in the morning. To get my daughter dressed and out the door to a park, where the backdrop was perfect for a picture. And once I was at the park, there were other mothers there, trying to figure out parenting, too.

The more pictures I took, the better I felt. It helped me focus. Feel close to her, even with the camera between us. Capture the beauty of what I had created, even if I still struggled to make sense of it.

And while I enjoyed being around my child, loved her, wanted good things for her, I still didn't feel that life-changing bond I was told I would feel the minute she emerged from my body.

Until one day, when Lowery was about two months old.

Like a robot, I went to get her out of her crib one morning, brought her back to our bed and handed her to Jim. When I placed her beside him she was immediately soothed. I remember looking at them and thinking that I need to snap out of it. I should feel my heart swell just looking at my loving husband and my beautiful daughter lying in bed cuddling on a lazy Sunday morning. Instead, I felt terrified I'd never get to the point of feeling better, being bonded, loving motherhood.

But something made me go get the camera. Go through the motions of snapping a few pictures of the two of them lying there together. And I began to cheer up slightly as I watched her nestle, snuggle, and even smile slightly, in the crook of her daddy's arm. And in that moment, there was a flash. A spark. The first feeling of happiness in weeks. And that feeling made me crawl in bed beside my husband and child. All three of us, on a quiet morning together in bed. Then I held the camera out and above our heads because I had a brilliant thought:

Take a picture.

It will last longer.

Extra! Extrovert!

My sister recently read the book, *Quiet: The Power of Introverts in a World That Can't Stop Talking.* This book spoke to my sister, an introvert herself, who has often felt powerless in a world full of extroverts. Ironically, my sister won't stop talking about this book.

I'm glad this book has given my sister a sense of belonging to a group of introverts who have long felt that they were getting the short end of the societal stick. It validated her feelings that extroverts are loud and overbearing and making everyone who is not an extrovert uncomfortable. But I've had to challenge her a bit about some of the book's content. Mostly, she seems to believe that introverts are the only ones who ever feel squeamish in certain social situations. She thinks that because I'm an extrovert, I don't ever feel awkward socially. And while I do not flinch at public speaking, or meeting new people, or talking to strangers, or hosting parties, there are a few occasions in everyday life that really make me uneasy.

Shoppers Beware

I really resent the plastic divider you have to place on the conveyer belt between your merchandise and the items of the customer in line ahead of you at the grocery store.

For starters, you almost always have to reach for it. You extend your arm—typically under the arms of a lady who's writing a check on that teeny check-writing pedestal—stretch out your hand to allow your finger tips to graze the plastic cube tube, and tickle it until it starts coming down the metal chute so you can get a firm grasp, at which point, you've attracted the attention of the check-writing customer.

This is when it gets worse. I feel the need to explain and apologize through facial expressions why I have to divide my groceries from hers. I need my toothpaste and mayonnaise not to touch your tortilla chips. And that's on me. Not you. I'm just particular. You're great.

And this sort of facial explanation inevitably causes me to begin talking compulsively with the customer, because I feel weird about drawing a line between our items as though I don't believe we are all brothers and sisters on this earth and only truly prosper when we share.

And when she seems not to understand why I'm yammering about how Kate Middleton—whose face covers the magazines in front of us—is doing a grave disservice to all new moms, I give up on her and turn to the customer behind me. I see that he is standing there with his groceries piled up on the metal edge of the conveyer belt, waiting for my condiments and diapers to move and give his purchases space.

So then I engage in the awkward reach again, this time for the second plastic divider, and place it between my groceries and his pile. And then I wonder if putting the divider between us is perceived as rude, because it's basically saying, "I, in no way, want to pay for your avocados." So then I start apologize/explain smiling and awkwardly commending him on his choice of mustard.

The Answer is No

More often than you would think, people will say "No" to a simple question you ask in an attempt to be playful. For example: I was in the copy room the other day, and a good friend was getting some extra paper for her office printer. I said, "Hey, can I borrow that stapler?" which was beside her. She said, "No, you cannot," and then smiled at me a second before handing it over.

There's always a beat in there before the person actually does whatever super easy task you've asked them to do. And in that beat, I'm left to respond in a way that accomplishes a few things: 1) playfully make it known I understand she's joking, 2) come back with something witty, as we are apparently engaged in banter, 3) use my will power not to punch her in the face.

Check, Please

I really struggle when I am out to lunch during the week with colleagues or community partners and the waiter says at the end of the meal, "Will this be one check, or shall I separate it?"

This makes me uncomfortable because it forces everyone at the table to play a game of ticket chicken. If you are the first to respond, you are admitting you are a tight ass who doesn't want to pay for anyone's meal but your own. If you are the last to respond, it looks like you were waiting for someone else to buy you lunch.

Happy Ending

I have sympathy awkwardness. I also project awkwardness that is usually accompanied by sympathy awkwardness. For example: I enjoy the occasional massage. But I struggle a bit with the ending.

No, no, not like that.

I project the awkwardness onto the masseuse when the massage has ended, and she has to tell me that it is over when I'm typically in the middle of a REM cycle. I'm lying naked under warm towels, the lights are off, music is playing, the fountain is tinkling, and I've been rubbed within an inch of my life (again, not like that, these are professionals). The massage is over but I don't know it. So the masseuse usually pats me lightly and says something like, "Okay, you're all done Meg."

I always startle a little and am tense because I wonder if I should have known it was over so she didn't have the awkward task of basically waking me up and telling me to pay her. And she may not find that awkward at all, but I project my awkwardness onto her, and then develop sympathy awkwardness and then start chatting incessantly about Kate Middleton.

Door to Door

I hate when people come to my door and try to sell something.
Mostly because the only way I know to avoid giving them a direct
answer is to revert to a 50s housewife mentality, claiming my
husband is the decision maker for the household.

And then I spend the remainder of the day mad at myself for
abandoning every single principle I hold dear by pretending my
vagina makes me incompetent just because I didn't want to tell
someone no.

Have a Drink

If you are a woman, and between the ages of 16 and 40, people
naturally assume you might be pregnant unless they see you
drinking a glass of wine, doing a line of coke or eating Feta cheese.
It's annoying to constantly be doing at least one of those just to
squelch a rumor.

Haggling

Sometimes, extroverts can make other extroverts uncomfortable
with all their extrovertedness. Recently, I helped my mother
furniture shop. She'd been looking for living room furniture for
nearly a year, and we finally found a few pieces she truly loved.

Instead of high fiving and going out for champagne, as I do for any
successful find, my mother prepared to haggle. I wrung my hands
and begged her not to, agreeing to personally pay her the amount
she was wanting off the couch and chairs if we could just walk out
of the store.

But she insisted, explaining that it's never about what you can
afford, it's about how much you should have to pay. So a spirited
back and forth between her and the salesman, with me pacing in the
background, resulted in a small victory for my mother, after which I
promptly went out to dry heave in my car. The car for which I
happily paid full sticker price.

Just Walk on By

I am extremely paranoid when someone walks behind me. This stems from a childhood spent with a severe limp. And though the limp has since been corrected, I still hold on to the paranoia that those walking behind me are wondering why I limp. In the mornings, before work, when I take a brisk walk in the park, I almost always come up against this problem. So much so that it's become increasingly clear that no one else suffers from this awkwardness, because so many people do it to me; they walk on the path directly behind me at the same pace so as never to pass me. And so, rather than spending my walk working through the problems of the day, or reconfiguring the furniture in our family room, I walk with my ass clenched tighter than a fist because I assume the jerk behind me is analyzing my gait.

Eye Contact

The close relative to my walking paranoia is passing someone head on in an extremely long hallway. The campus where I work was designed with an eye toward making people feel uncomfortable. The building is constructed of long narrow hallways with no open congregating spaces to break up all the awkwardness.

As I'm walking down the 100-yard hallway, I hold my breath if I see another soul coming toward me. If I make eye contact too quickly, then I feel the need to hold the gaze until the person passes. If I keep my head down to avoid premature eye contact, then I can't accurately judge the optimum window for looking up and smiling. But these are my only two options. I'm sure as hell not gonna turn around in the middle of the hall and walk the other way, because I don't want whoever it is watching my ass give itself a wedgie from clenching so hard.

Birthmark

When my oldest daughter Lowery was just three months old, she began to develop a faint birthmark by her left eye.

This excited me.

Babies are so pretty and pristine. New, fresh, painstakingly perfect. Now I not only had a beautiful, smooth, perfectly formed baby, but one with a distinguishing characteristic. An attribute that was hers and no one else's. Finally something that would give me a quick visual sign that she was *my* baby, so I would stop trying to leave day care with other people's babies in my arms. Seriously. They all look alike.

I also liked that she had this particular birthmark because I had several of the same kind scattered across my body. These marks are just slightly darker than my natural skin tone, and they only appear after some extended period of sun exposure. I have one on my wrist that looks like the Virgin Islands, and one on my chest that looks like Wisconsin.

Lowery's, however, was far more striking and glorious than my American marks. As she aged and spent more time at the park, we began to notice hers was an exact replica of Africa.

On the middle of her bottom left eyelid is Algeria. Sierra Leone sits where her cheek raises for a smile and it sweeps beautifully off to the side of her face, with Angola, Namibia and the far southern tip reaching down just to the bottom of her cheek bone. And, with amazing geographical accuracy, she has another smaller spot just south and east of Mozambique: Madagascar.

This birthmark is only faintly noticeable when you first look at her. Most flashes on cameras completely wash it out. When she spends a few days indoors it almost disappears. But when she faces the sun while splashing around in her kiddie pool, or waddles around the backyard, it begins to appear, ever so slightly darker than her normally golden skin. And mine appear, as I sit beside her in the sun, and I'm warmed by the thought that we are bursting with colors together.

It never occurred to me that anyone would look upon this beautiful mark as anything but a representation of my child's own uniqueness and her genetic connection to her mother. But it should have.

Because people can suck.

When I was eight years old I was in a horrific car accident. Aside from broken bones and blurry vision, my face was severely mangled by the gravel and brush alongside the road that I landed on after being thrown clear of the car.

I underwent extremely invasive facial surgery to repair the right side of my face, my chin and my forehead. And though the doctors did meticulous and brilliant work, they left me with a patch of new, bright pink flesh on my cheek and told me it would never have freckles like the rest of my face.

A gaping wound on the top of my forehead looked like old, minced, wrinkled flesh, and the gash on my chin—that runs vertically from the left side of my bottom lip—would be a scar I'd have to learn to live with.

Don't worry, this story has the happiest of endings. Buck up.

Over time, the wrinkly wound on my forehead moved up into my hair, and I really have to search along my hairline to even feel it anymore. The pinkness of my cheek faded within a few years and— despite the doctor's medical opinion—freckles grew rampantly, blending in almost seamlessly with the rest of my rampant freckles.

By the time I reached high school, the scar on my chin faded to the pale shade of the rest of my face. The swollen, bumpy scar tissue subsided so that it no longer looked like I needed a spittoon. And while there is still a large scar there, it's pretty easy to cover most of it with a touch of makeup. I don't even notice it anymore when I look in the mirror.

But just because I fail to see it doesn't mean others don't notice. For years, while I was still extremely traumatized by the car accident, strangers in stores would come up to my mother and her young, scar-faced daughter and say, "What happened to her?" I don't actually know how my mother handled these moments because I always took off walking in a different direction, leaving her to defend me.

When I got older, strangers stopped asking my mother and started asking me. "What's wrong with your face?" One woman even asked me if I had severe poison ivy. And if so, to stay away from her.

Yes. People can suck.

And they can feel an extreme sense of entitlement by noticing something different about you and demanding you give them an explanation.

But over time I came to field these kinds of questions quite well. "Oh, it's an old wound from a car accident 15 years ago." Or, "Bar fight." Or, silently, "Go fuck yourself."

Hearing the question still makes my eyes hot. I'm not sure that will ever go away. But even if it never does, I've accomplished the impossible. I fought through trauma *and* the vanities of junior high, and I've learned to like my face.

So I shouldn't have been surprised when the 90-year-old salesclerk at the craft store looked at my sweet, precious daughter, who was saying "Hi!" and waving feverishly, and exclaimed "Dear God! What happened to her face?"

I stopped dead.

"What do you mean?" I asked tersely.

"Looks like she has a black eye. Was she injured?"

"It's a birthmark. Certainly you've seen one before," I shot back at her.

"I meant nothing by it," she said flatly. "It just looks like she got hit."

So not only was she pointing out my child was different, but also possibly accusing me of child abuse.

I could have refused to shop there, I guess. Or called the manager. Or waited in the parking lot after her shift and jumped her. But that would not take away from other questions Lowery might get every summer when her beautiful continent appears on her perfect face.

A few days later, at Lowery's one-year check up, the doctor commented on her birthmark. I puffed up and shot at her: "It's beautiful."

She laughed and said, "Yes, I agree. Gives her character."

I sighed with relief until she asked, "But does she have any others?"

I looked at her strangely and explained that she has a very small one that resembles Saudi Arabia on her right butt cheek, and an even teenier one that looks vaguely like Iceland on her hip. I inquired why she even asked.

Turns out that six or more of the types of birthmarks that Lowery and I have can be a sign of neurofibromatosis. Which is a frightening disorder in which a child develops tumors on her nerves. To rule out the possibility, the doctor used a small tape measure and scoured my squirming daughter's body to try to see the faint spots well enough to measure them for a total number of birthmark centimeters.

Before I could panic, the doctor explained that birthmarks, 90 percent of the time, are genetic. She asked if I had similar marks. When I tried to unbutton my pants and rip off my bra, she said she believed me and there was no need to show her.

She also said that neurofibromatosis has other telltale signs, like being delayed in speech (Lowery started talking at eight months and hasn't stopped since), or a small head (no need to quote what percentile she's in; my vagina can confirm its mass), and we have no history of it on either side of our family. And even if she were the 1 child in 4000 who has this, there is nothing we can do until she's at least five years old.

But Lowery's doing just fine. Talks excitedly to every stranger in the grocery store. Kisses anyone who will stand still long enough. Talks in her sleep. Wants nothing in this world but to be read to and tickled and to eat her weight in goldfish crackers.

I'm not going to let the rude questions of strangers, or the inquiries of my overly cautious doctor, distract me from my first thoughts about my child's health and beauty. And I won't let the trauma of my past be projected onto my child. Questions about her birthmark may not ever bother Lowery. There's not a traumatic story behind her lovely mark. It's not a sensitive subject for her. Though it's inevitable she'll grow up with her own touchy subjects, like we all do. Go ahead, ask me if I breastfed or how much older my husband is.

I know with certainty Lowery will grow up to be brilliant, accomplished, witty, compassionate, thoughtful and loved. And maybe one day she'll visit Africa and feel so connected that she'll live there, make change there and maybe, just maybe, raise a daughter there.

But for now I can damn sure guarantee how I'll handle the next sales lady who rudely suggests my child's birthmark is anything less than glorious.

I'll leave a mark on her ass, shaped very much like Italy.

You Can't Ignore Your Past

This summer, my good friend Elizabeth got married on her parents' land in our hometown. Given the nature of our small town, most everyone from our past was set to come. And sometimes, facing your past is difficult. Even with two layers of Spanx.

Elizabeth is a world traveler, if not, perhaps, a professional nomad. She's lived and traveled all over and has picked up numerous interesting and dynamic friends along the way.

Her wedding was much like an international airport, with strangers from around the world uniting for a common purpose. Her friends from her current life in D.C., friends from her many international travels, friends from her time in law school, friends from camp and college, and her friends, of course, from our hometown.

Though it quickly became evident there was a divide among Elizabeth's friends: everyone after high school knows her only as *Liz*.

Upon meeting all of her new friends, they would ask how I knew Liz. I would say that I didn't know Liz, but I knew *Elizabeth* quite well. When I used her full name, they would say, "Oh, you must have gone to high school together." But in our town, saying you "went to high school together" is like saying you climbed the last three feet of Kilimanjaro's peak.

I *grew up* with Elizabeth. Our parents were best friends before we were ever born. We sold Girl Scout cookies together, were in the same dance class, had sleepovers, got our driver's licenses together, went to prom together, met every Sunday for breakfast while she was in law school, and my mother made her wedding cake, as well as the wedding cake for her sister, who married my cousin, whom she met at my wedding.

But, yes, I suppose we did also go to high school together.

Those who know *Elizabeth* remember her as organized, smart, studious and ambitious. Always in t-shirts, jeans and glasses, with her hair styled in a straight, chin length bob. Those who met *Liz* know the easy-going free spirit with the contact lenses, flawlessly chic clothing and long, flowing, wavy hair.

The wedding weekend was a festival of events. A bachelorette party, rehearsal and rehearsal dinner, post rehearsal dinner party, bonfire, bridal brunch, professional photo shoot, wedding, reception, photo booth, lighting of the Wish Lanterns and the post-wedding hangover.

This provided ample time to meet new people. Most of whom didn't personally know of Elizabeth's past in our hometown. Which meant they also didn't know of mine. They were meeting the Meg who was a married mother with a career. They didn't know of the Past Meg, who was once inexplicably into reggae music and wore a lot of tie-dye. And this is what is so exhilarating about meeting new people. Fresh start every time. Introduce yourself with control of the information.

But you can't ignore your past. Because it always shows up to weddings.

After the rehearsal dinner, guests were treated to a slideshow presentation, in which we watched Elizabeth evolve into Liz.

One picture caught me by surprise: a picture of Elizabeth and me at graduation, in our caps and gowns, clutching our diplomas while hugging each other around the neck. Elizabeth's eyes were glassy, puffy and red. Mine were bright and happy. I turned to my good friend Lindsey and asked if she had cried at our high school graduation. She leaned in and whispered, "I think you were the only one who didn't."

There I was, in the picture, unmoved by the thought of leaving high school. Meanwhile, my classmates around me, the people I'd grown up with, seemed like this was a tragic end to something. It was only in that moment, 10 years later, married with a child, that I felt a pang for my past.

During the bridal brunch the next day, one of Liz's friends asked what I was like in high school. I explained using words like "gothic" and "slutty" and "boozehound." She seemed somewhat convinced, until one of Elizabeth's friends interjected, "Meg was the same then as she is now!"

Especially my hair.

Last week the fall semester began, which marks my fourth year— and fourteenth class—teaching as an adjunct. I walked into my upper level division Ethics class and scanned the room. Some students I had seen before in the hallways, others I knew by reputation. A few had been in my class the previous semester. But mostly, as I prefer it, there was a room full of fresh new faces staring back at me. But after introductions and once I started the lecture, the door flew open and in walked a very familiar face. A girl named Tracy. I remembered her from the first course I ever taught.

When she was originally in my class, four years ago, she was impossibly thin, had dark hair streaked with bleach, and wore braces on her teeth. Back then she sat on the front row, wore pathetically short shorts and low cut tops, and smacked her gum through my lectures. She talked a lot, too. She often blurted out thoughtless comments that brought on muffled laughter from the rows behind her. And while I typically defend everyone's opinion in my class, even I shuddered when she announced one day that she would never have children because she didn't want to "lose her body."

"Remember me?" she asked as she took a seat near the back.

Of course I did. Except I noticed she had filled out just slightly, giving her a healthy glow. She was wearing a nice dress of appropriate length. Her hair was a natural color. And her braces were gone. She looked so much older to me in that moment that I wondered what she thought of my appearance. If I looked different to her.

Except for my hair.

I prepared myself for her childish comments during my lecture. I prepared myself to have to break up her whispering to a friend during class. I was even prepared to stay after every week to help her further with the material.

But then a funny thing happened. She listened attentively to my lecture. She took notes. And she raised her hand to interject a comment while the class discussed the ethical dilemma of politicians who get caught sexting. She spoke with confidence and made a compelling argument for the problems of political figures losing public trust. And she didn't laugh once when she said "Anthony Weiner."

Even I couldn't manage that.

After class she came up and gave me a hug. She said she was thrilled to see me again, and that she had heard from others who had taken my classes that I had finished my PhD and had a baby since I last saw her. She mentioned that she herself had gotten married, becoming a stepmother in the process, and had been given a promotion at work, which prompted her to finally declare a major. Standing in front of me was a truly poised and beautiful woman. She asked a few questions about the upcoming assignment, thanked me for my time, and walked gracefully out of the classroom.

Moments later she poked her head back in and said, "Oh! *Weiner.* Like a man's wiener! I just now got that! Hilarious!"

That moment reminded me of the car ride home from Elizabeth's wedding. I was telling my husband how meeting all of Elizabeth's new friends was a relief. When he asked why, I explained that I was worried she had changed too much. Or that the Elizabeth I knew was gone. Replaced by Liz. But in meeting Liz's friends, it was obvious that she, at her core, was the same remarkable person she's always been.

Then I recounted all the many great conversations I had with my former high school classmates, some of whom I hadn't seen in years. And I began to cry.

"What's wrong?" he asked. "Why are you crying?"

"I miss them," I shrugged.

Which made me feel a bit better. Because the only thing worse than people from your past thinking you are nothing like they remember you, is having them think:

You haven't changed a bit.

Next Steps

Ⅰf you were to ask me if my family is a competitive bunch, I would struggle to respond. Mostly because my mother would try to answer first.

My family's competitive nature comes out in less than conventional ways. Number of books read (me). Trivial Pursuit winner (my brother). Best margarita recipe (tough call). Rarely, if ever, does it involve sports. Or money. Or success.

The latest competition my family has engaged in is the high stakes, thrill-a-minute, edge of your seat world of walking. More specifically, a pedometer device called the FitBit. This little gizmo works like a pedometer, but in a much more intuitive way. There are no buttons to push, and it automatically resets at midnight. The model I purchased counts steps, miles and calories burned in a day. Higher end models, like the ones my parents and siblings have, also monitor sleeping patterns. The most expensive model will check insulin levels and keep tabs on your 401(k).

When my FitBit arrived in the mail, I was surprised to find it's about the size of a quarter. It fits nicely into a little silicone clip that can be worn in your pocket. But, due to my vast array of dresses and yoga pants, I've opted to wear my FitBit on my bra. Right smack in the middle of the cleave. For me, when worn there, it practically disappears.

The FitBit also has a digital face: two eyes and a mouth. And he smiles bigger and bigger the more active I am throughout the day. Inactivity earns me squinty eyes and a wagging tongue. The FitBit syncs wirelessly to my iPhone. And it comes with its own social network. If Facebook is the site that makes you feel you aren't stacking up as a cook or a mother, Fitbit's network is the one that makes you feel like a lazy piece of shit.

The goal, as the Japanese brilliantly marketed back in the 90s in an attempt to sell pedometers, is to walk at least 10,000 steps a day. This is the equivalent of 5 miles. The average person with a desk job gets in somewhere between 2,000 and 4,000 steps a day. To get 10,000 one needs to add in some intentional exercise, like a brisk walk. Medical research posits that continual, low impact activity throughout the day is greater than, say, a turbo charged Zumba class—which I've never taken, but I think it involves cage fighting in trash bags.

The first week I wore my FitBit my family was traveling for our annual vacation at a sprawling lake house. At that time, my parents and my sister had been wearing their FitBits for several weeks. The first morning I awoke to find my mother, father and sister quietly eating breakfast. My brother was doing yoga on the deck. My sister-in-law was cleaning dishes.

I joined in for waffles and then excused myself to take a shower. When I finished showering and drying my hair, I came out of the bathroom to a deserted house. I looked on the back deck, in all the bedrooms, in the living room and in every closet. My family had vanished. I panicked. I knew the only plausible explanation for their disappearance, but I just couldn't allow myself to believe it.

Those competitive sons of bitches were out for a walk.

When we returned home from our trip, I received news that our child was finally given a full-time slot at day care, after waiting six months (her) and countless bottles of wine (me).

Colors seemed brighter.

The two most overwhelming stresses in my life—staying at home with Lowery and graduate school—both came to a close within a month of each other. If the FitBit measured skips taken through fields of flowers, I'd win. So with those two problems finding solutions simultaneously, I was able to think differently about my life. My daily routine. What my next steps were going to be.

My parents walk constantly as part of their professions. My father, a large animal veterinarian, is always on his feet, as bulls do not often come and sit in his lap while he measures their scrotal circumference. My mother, an entrepreneurial caterer, moves about her commercial kitchen all day long to the hum of the Food Network. Both can reach 10,000 steps before noon. My brother is a competitive canoe racer, but the FitBit doesn't care about arm movement.

This leaves my sister as my only real competition.

As an engineer, her job couldn't be more sedentary. She sits in front of a computer, or drafting table, or train caboose—I don't know specifically what she does at work, but I know it doesn't require much walking. But that doesn't matter because my sister always has to win. For the past two weeks she's been beating the veterinarian who walked hundreds of acres to pregnancy check 800 head of cattle, and the caterer who served 700 people at a sit down dinner, because she finds ways to work in the steps. Not for her health. Not for her heart. But for the love of the game.

Mostly the winning part of the game.

And then there's me. Dead last, but only by a couple hundred steps each day. I hit 10,000, sometimes eleven, every day. And there are two reasons why I can hit these numbers now: 1) I've graduated, and 2) my child is in full-time day care.

School and the dissertation kept me glued to a classroom seat or stuck in front of a computer for hours on end. And while it would make more sense that days with my child were more active than days without her, it's simply not the case. It surprised me to find that I walk more, a lot more, when I'm not at home with my child.

Chasing after a toddler is exhausting, but it isn't always cardiovascular. Often it's sitting down for pretend tea, while she circles laps around me. Or scrubbing dried cottage cheese off the kitchen floor. Or standing by the door yelling for her to come get in the car while she runs like mad around the house gathering up dolls to take with us. Being home may be mentally exhausting but, apparently, not terribly physically demanding.

But in the one week she's been in full-time day care, a lot about my life has changed. I'm calmer. Less stressed. More fulfilled at work. Pooping by myself more often. And, apparently, walking a lot.

Because I'm a Myers and competition is in my genes—fighting off other perfectly good traits—I don't want to be too far behind the steps of my father, mother and sister. I strive to rack up a winning number so that I can impress my parents, silence my sister and get a smile out of a device wedged between my tits.

For the past few weeks I've been measuring the success of my day in steps taken. I often march in place during Lowery's bath if I've not yet reached goal. It's thrilling to get credit for every step I take. Even if the steps are into the kitchen to get a cookie. I feel like I've accomplished something every day when I get a wide, manic smile from my FitBit. And its mere presence in my undergarment reminds me to move more.

But it's impossible to forget that I'm moving more because I'm with Lowery less.

Don't get me wrong, I want her in full-time day care despite how much I miss her. Just like regardless of how much I miss the challenge of school, I don't want to be a student again. And while I sometimes wish my family could be pacifists, I'll bet I wouldn't have accomplished as much in my life if it weren't for the inherent taste for blood.

And to make a better margarita than my brother.

Everything's a trade off. Less Lowery equals more of everything else. And when I start to feel like that balance is tilting too far, and I want to jerk her out of day care, quit my job and stay home with her, I have a simple solution:

I walk it off.

Rejected

During my senior year of high school, my parents told me they would happily take me to tour any colleges in which I might have an interest. So I asked them to drive me 10 hours to a little town three states away. The college is renowned for its creative writing program, its award-winning library and its high national ranking in overall pretentiousness.

We loaded up my parents' Suburban and drove north until we hit snow. When we arrived on campus, we were greeted by a tall, skinny junior, with long, dirty hair, wearing shorts, flip flops and a hoodie that read, "Privatize This" with a picture of a brain on it. With the straightest of expressions he introduced himself as "Pear." I was irked when my father chuckled. Even more so when he said, "I'm sorry, Perry is it?"

"No," said Pear. "It's *Pear*. Like the fruit."

Pear took us around the campus and showed us the art studios, the writing labs, the expressive yoga rooms, the reading lofts and the cafeteria that served mostly vegan foods. When he walked us across the Quad he took his shoes off so his "toes could be one with the grass." We passed a couple making out on a hemp blanket, and a guitar-playing loner, who was, according to Pear, the Poetry Department Chair.

After our campus tour, I was scheduled to be interviewed by the Dean of Admissions, who had reviewed my application and was "decently impressed" with my entrance essay, but thought meeting me would help the committee make its final decision. I left my parents with Pear to—as I can only assume—smoke a bowl, and went into my two-hour interview.

Many of the questions were well above my knowledge base, but I was able to give her honest and profound reflections on the latest Jonathan Franzen novel, and I nailed the question about the nation's abuse of the semicolon. I walked away knowing that, while I may not have been perfect, I had done the best I could.

When we left campus, Pear waving to us in the rearview mirror, I knew one thing: I wanted to be accepted.

And so, back at home, I waited.

And waited.

Until one day, months after our visit, I received a very flat envelope with the college's logo in the top left corner. They regretted to inform me, but they did not think I was a good fit for their program.

No nationally renowned writing program. No award-winning library. No making out with Pear, wearing ponchos, while our friends played hackie sack to the music our poetry professor belted out across the Quad.

I had been rejected.

My father was uncomfortable with my sadness. He wanted nothing more than to move past this misfortune and continue on with more campus tours.

My mother, on the other hand, was vengeful. She took the letter, pressed it out flat and read it over and over and over. Then she opened the file folder in which she kept only the most important of documents, which included all her children's birth certificates and her tomato torte recipe, and laid the letter on top.

"Mom, why are you keeping that?" I asked through tears.

"For when you make it big, darling. I can give this to Oprah."

Yes, my mother kept that rejection letter so that Oprah would one day sit next to me on her sparkling white couch and hold my hand and say, "I cannot believe *you*, a person beloved by *millions*, the richest, most successful woman in all the world, was once rejected by a small, liberal arts college in a cornfield! I *just* can't believe it!" And this would inevitably spark a boycott of the college, as fervent as the beef boycott she sparked in the 90s, which would ultimately force the institution to close due to its wild unpopularity spurred by universal loyalty to me.

Later, when I settled on another college with a strong writing program, I was encouraged by my professors to submit my writings for publication. I sent out numerous essays to various literary journals and magazines all over the nation. I received 22 rejection letters all saying the same thing:

No thanks.

Rejection wasn't just confined to my writing aspirations. I once professed (mentioned in passing) my deep love (moderate appreciation) for a guy I met at college who responded by saying, "You're nice, but I'm looking for someone more domestic to settle down with."

I was rejected by two PhD programs before I was accepted into the one I completed. I produced about a year's worth of negative pregnancy tests, and endured a failed round of fertility treatments before I became pregnant. And now, in the middle of my post-doctorate job search, I'm getting rejected left and right.

But most recently, the rejection I'm struggling the hardest with is of a more personal nature. This past month, my child has transitioned to full-time day care, and I'm back at work. This is a radical transformation from the first two years of her life, during which we spent most every day, all day, together.

But in the move to full-time day care I've noticed that she's showing subtle signs of struggling with all the change. She's become needier.

For her father.

At night she wants Daddy to brush her teeth and read to her. In the mornings she wants Daddy to pick out her clothes. She wants Daddy to rock her dolls, and Daddy to run through the sprinklers with her.

Recently, she took a tumble and hit her head on the hardwood floors. The kind of fall that you know by sound alone was bad. Jim and I both rushed to her side, but she immediately reached for him. I tried to join in the hug, desperate to offer my love and support, but she shook me off. Slapped at me to go away and buried her face in Jim's chest. My typical remedy of kissing her boo-boo and scolding the hard surface she collided with was not what she wanted. She wanted her father.

This destroyed me.

And my feelings about this surprised me. It contradicted the pride I have in her extreme independence. How I love that she springs out of my arms when I drop her off at school while other children claw at their parents' necks, screaming dramatically. How I revel in the fact that my child is self-possessed, confident, strong-willed and wildly independent. So in that moment when she rejected my love, I started crying alongside my hurting child, who wouldn't let me kiss her, wouldn't let me touch her, wouldn't let me make it better.

It was momentary. After a few minutes, she was on the couch, brushing my hair out and caking pretend makeup on my face. But I couldn't shake the feeling of the first moment my child made a choice about which parent she wanted, *needed,* and she didn't choose me.

There's really nothing that makes rejection sting less. It's rotten to be told you aren't the right person, or you don't qualify, or you weren't a good fit, or you aren't the one, or you didn't try hard enough.

Because the moment you decide to pursue something—college, a job, parenthood—you imagine yourself in the desired outcome. You picture your new dorm room, or new office, or growing belly, and you start to believe it's already true.

And so, when the news comes that your desires won't be met, that your dreams won't come to fruition, it's hard not to grieve the loss of the life you thought you would have. And that's the worst part of it: you have no control. All you can really do is accept the rejection.

Even if you do it in irrational ways.

Like how my mother has held on to my rejection letter all these years. It's still there, yellowing in a folder, waiting for me to make it something of extreme irony.

I realize now that she wasn't really doing that for me, though I think she still truly believes I can somehow stick it to the college through Oprah. She was doing it for herself. As a mother. Trying to do something for her hurting daughter when nothing could really be done. Which assures me that despite all the rejection I might endure in this lifetime, there's one acceptable upside:

At least someone is keeping my information on file.

A Natural Occurrence

In college I drove a fluorescent teal, 10-year-old Jeep Cherokee. It made funny noises, was missing a hub cap, and didn't have cup holders. But I loved that car because it was so distinctive.

One morning I found the driver's side door covered in sap. I thought parking next to a tree would have kept my vehicle cool in the hot Missouri summer, but the stickiness on my car hardly seemed worth the cooler temperature.

For a couple of days I drove around with the gooey mess on the side of my Day-Glo vehicle. While parked on campus one afternoon, a friend walked by and commented on the stain. I nodded sheepishly and said, "Yeah, I parked by a tree and it got covered in sap." I saw something flash in my friend's eyes.

Was it doubt? Was it pity?

And standing with him on the sidewalk, a little farther from my car than I was when I first noticed the goo, I looked over to the driver's door and saw the full outline of the stain for the first time. It was concentrated on the door, in a very specific spot, and then fanned out from the center, with streaks extending up to the top of the driver's window and down to the tread on the tires. And when I saw this, I realized instantly that the dried liquid wasn't tree sap. It was Coke. And the splatter pattern indicated the Coke had been intentionally—even angrily—hurled at the driver's side door of a very recognizable vehicle.

I had very much misread the situation.

When I became pregnant with my second child, my husband and I sat down with a list of tasks we'd like to accomplish before the baby was born. This is a silly endeavor, of course, as it fools parents into a false sense of preparedness.

There were a few predictable tasks on the list, like painting the nursery, buying diapers and car shopping. But there were three specific tasks on the list that gave me great anxiety, as they were all focused on my darling, almost-three-year-old who was naively excited to become a big sister.

1) Take away the pacifier.
2) Potty train.
3) Transition out of the crib.

These tasks would require patience, diligence, care and time. I was clear to my husband that I wanted these to roll out in phases so as not to upset our child with too much change at once. We had a nine month window to complete our tasks.

Take Away the Pacifier

Our child was never truly obsessed with the pacifier, and really only ever wanted it at naps and bedtime. But around her second birthday she took to hoarding every pacifier she owned, needing them to be in the crib with her each night. She would suck on one and arrange the others in interesting shapes, or lay them on the mouths of the dolls that surrounded her.

I was somewhat concerned that her recent attachment to them was the result of something deeper—perhaps she was struggling with a problem at school, or was fearful of growing up—and I worried that taking them away from her might be a harrowing, and potentially damaging, action.

As it goes with any parents trying to take away the pacifier, my husband and I wanted to find the perfect moment. So we had to wait until she was over a cold. Then after her birthday. Then after she adjusted to daylight savings time. After the World Series. It was maddening trying to find the perfect night to strip her of the nine pacifiers with which she had grown accustomed to sleeping.

But then, one Saturday morning, we went to the zoo. She decided on that beautiful, sunny day—somewhere near the elephants—to throw a massive tantrum. So, in a moment of sheer desperation, while we were buckling her in the car as she kicked and screamed, I sternly said to her, "Okay, no binkie at nap time!"

My husband and I got in the front seat and just stared at each other. What had I done? Our child sat motionless in her car seat. We drove home in silence, all three of us fearing the impending pacifier-less nap.

At home, as we laid our child in her crib, she looked up at us and asked, "Okay, so no binkie?" I looked at my husband and he nodded.

"Yes…" I said less firmly than before. "No binkie." We closed her door, walked down the stairs and stood there fighting in the quiet manner parents have perfected.

Was it the right time? What should we do if she refused to nap? Isn't sleep more important than the task? Is taking it away as a punishment going to make her think her prized possessions are collateral? Should we go buy a book about this or something? Google it, maybe?

While we silently argued at the bottom of the stairs for a solid fifteen minutes, we failed to notice that our child hadn't made a noise. We crept up the stairs, opened her door and found her sleeping soundly.

She never mentioned her pacifier again.

Potty Train

We purchased an Elmo Training Potty for our child to slowly acclimate her to the idea of using one. But instead of wanting to "use" it, she wanted to play with it.

She constantly fiddled with the handle, which produced the sound of Elmo giggling maniacally. She put her Legos in the basin. She balanced her sippy cups on the tank. Basically, it was just another thing crowding the bathroom.

We had decided potty training needed to be a gentle process that she would lead. We wanted to wait a few months after taking away the pacifier before we even mentioned the words "potty training" to her. And much like our plan with the pacifier, we wanted to find the perfect time to start the process. Which meant we definitely needed to wait until my husband came home from an overseas trip. So we decided that when he returned from Belgium, we would see if she was ready.

My daughter and I drove my husband to the airport at seven in the morning in the middle of an ice storm, double-checked that he had his passport, kissed him goodbye, and drove carefully back home. The moment we walked through the front door, my child put her hands on her hips and said, "I'd like to go pee in the potty."

Still in my coat, and sad from having said goodbye to my husband, I dragged her Elmo Potty out of the bathroom and into the middle of the living room floor. She pulled off her snow boots, stripped off her pants, unfastened her diaper and sat forcefully down on the potty. While I was taking off my scarf I heard a tiny stream of liquid hitting the plastic bin.

My child stood up, stretched out her arms in victory and exclaimed, "I did it! I did it!" I peered into the tiny potty to find it half full of my child's urine, and I screamed out in excitement. My child, completely naked—with snow falling outside the window—ran around the living room clapping and giggling.

She didn't wait until her father returned home. She didn't wait until we deliberately started the process with her. She didn't even wait for me to take off my coat. She just decided she needed to go, got naked and went.

Transition Out of the Crib

Having accidentally (though successfully) taken away the pacifiers, and having watched our daughter spontaneously (though impressively) learn to pee in the potty, we felt she was ready to transition out of the crib.

I worried about this one the most. I decided we would leave the crib in her room for the first two weeks because I thought that seeing the crib might comfort her during this transition. And if we had a successful first two weeks, I had another plan: I found an adorable child-sized desk and chair so as to replace the crib with something positive, rather than leave a vacant spot in her room. Or, I dunno, a hole in her heart.

Last Friday night, after talking about it all week, it was time for our daughter to finally sleep in her big girl bed. She came home from school asking if it was bedtime. She talked all through dinner about which direction she could sleep on the bed, what blanket she planned to use, and which dolls she wanted with her. After brushing her teeth and helping her into pajamas, I put our child on the bed. She snuggled into the pillows, arranged her dolls closely to her body, and pulled the blanket up to her chin. She looked at us and smiled. "I'm a big girl," she said, through a yawn.

We both kissed her goodnight and quietly left. When we got to the bottom of the stairs, my husband turned around to find me crying without restraint. He held me, half concerned, half laughing.

I laughed through my tears, too, because I had so clearly misread the situation.

Like the brown, sticky stain on my car door in college.

I thought what had happened was simply a natural occurrence: sap dripping from a tree. But in actuality, it was an anonymous enemy expressing anger at me. And my daughter, having just been curled up in her crib—wearing a diaper, sucking on a pacifier—was now tucked happily under blankets on a bed I bought before she was born. Despite how much I anticipated her growth, and how meticulously I prepared for it, I felt like I was seeing her growing outline clearly for the first time.

Even though her growth is a natural occurrence, it certainly feels like an angry enemy.

And I'm just now seeing it.

The Loch Ness Monster

During my semester abroad in college, three of my friends and I signed up for a weeklong adventure tour around Scotland. This mostly involved hiking across the Scottish countryside and visiting castles and distilleries with 20 strangers from all over the world. The last stop on our tour was Loch Ness, where we hoped to catch a glimpse of the massive, magical monster I secretly believed was real.

As our rickety tour bus lumbered over the hills and valleys, toward the water, our tour guide Ruthie—a short brunette with a Scottish brogue—began telling about the first time she visited Loch Ness.

She and her two best friends grew up hearing about the loch's mystical powers, powers provided by the beautiful and elusive Monster, in whom the natives aggressively believe. The lore suggests that pursuing the Loch Ness Monster is, in and of itself, a measure of true bravery. And so, it is believed that to show your certainty in the Monster, and your valiant efforts to find her, you should run naked into the loch. Don't think about how deep the water is (one of the deepest lakes in the world) or how cold the water is (such deep waters can't get warm in the misty Scotland climate). Just run. Dive deep down into the endless, frigid waters, and when you come out, you come out cloaked with good fortune as a reward for your courage and faith.

Then you toast your new luck with a swig of Scotland's finest drink.

Ruthie laughed fondly as she told of how she and her friends emerged from the loch, naked and shivering, and spent the evening warming by a fire while they sipped whiskey and watched the waves carry all their bad luck out to sea. She couldn't explain how, exactly, but that night changed her life. When the dawn came and the whiskey hangover subsided, she knew she would never be the same.

She seemed lost in her memories as we were pulling up to the water's edge. She turned off the engine, reached under her seat, pulled out an unopened bottle of Scotch, and glanced back at everyone on the bus.

Without looking at each other, without even uttering a word, my friends and I, in beautiful synchronization, kicked off our shoes and began unbuttoning our shirts. We were stumbling off the bus as we unzipped our pants. We hopped around on the rocks trying to pull the socks from our feet. And on that cold, foggy Scotland day—like some beautiful, slow motion scene in a gripping movie about a dog finding its way home—we all ran toward the water.

When my feet first hit the water, an icy chill went through my entire body in a painful jolt. Though I felt frozen, my body kept moving over the slippery, smooth pebbles that cover the loch's floor. I kept running. I ran until I was up to my neck in frigid water.

And then I dove.

Once I completely submerged my entire body in the wintery water, I popped up immediately, a little surprised to be alive. I quickly and effortlessly swam back to shore. And there was Ruthie, jumping and screaming with delight as she waved her siren bottle of Scotch in the air. She ran to us, enveloping us all in a joyful embrace. We were all leaping in the air and triumphantly high-fiving while Ruthie cracked open the bottle. As we gathered up our clothes, which had made a trail from the bus to the shore, we looked up to notice, for the first time, that the rest of the tour group was still on the bus, faces pressed against the windows, mouths agape.

In that moment, all I wanted was to make my college years last forever.

A few weeks ago, I received a job offer to become a faculty member at a major university. While this is great news and I couldn't be more excited by the opportunity, this job offer was the end result of an extremely long hunt.

While in the midst of my dissertation research, had been speculation around campus that a faculty position might be opening up in my field of study. At the time, it was just a rumor. Mere myth. For months I tried to find out more information. I'd casually ask people in the break room. I'd eavesdrop on conversations in the bathroom. I'd stand with my ear suctioned to a cup pressed up to the dean's door.

To me, the rumored position—and all the details about it that I liberally filled in myself—seemed wonderful. While I've never subscribed to the notion of a "dream job" it certainly fit many criteria for the kind of job I'd want. This mythical opportunity could allow me the challenging career I've long desired, coupled with the flexibility I would need with a family. And it's no secret that opportunities for newly minted PhDs are a very grim fairy-tale.

Over the course of two years, my life accidentally became a prolonged quest for this folkloric possibility. Despite having no factual evidence that this job would ever exist, or if I'd even be considered for it, I carried on ambitiously as though it did and I would.

It wasn't as if I wasted time while I waited. I birthed and cared for a child while I finished my doctorate degree. Then I became pregnant with another child. I worked as an adjunct teacher and as a researcher on various grant-funded projects for the university. I did a fair amount of consultation work. I had the dog groomed. But I found myself refusing to settle into a permanent position.

At first, I felt courageous. Believing in the existence of something without reason or evidence. But in the meantime, I let many other opportunities pass me by. I even turned down an incredibly gracious job offer, one that would have really benefited my family financially, for the absurd pursuit of what was basically folklore.

Waiting was not only making me crazy, it was making me selfish.

After more than a year of fantasizing, the rumored opening became fact. A national search was to be held to fill the role. And a search can take up to a year as candidates from across the country are vetted and considered. Though I knew internal candidates are rarely chosen in academics, I applied and prepared myself for another extended wait.

Another year went by.

All the waiting created a certain level of self-doubt. And depression. Well-intentioned friends kept asking if I had heard anything, and my explanation for still waiting made me feel irrational, manic even. But eventually, just as I was about to give up, the waiting turned into progress. And the progress turned into an interview. And the interview turned into an offer. And the offer turned into a job.

As I prepared to start my new role as an Assistant Professor, I wondered what I'm sure the Scottish have always secretly wondered: could the monster ever be as magical as it has been imagined?

That afternoon in Scotland—after we emerged from the water, caught our breath, and got dressed—we stumbled, fuzzy from whiskey, over to a silver Airstream parked close to shore. A sign outside read: Loch Ness Monsters For Sale £1.00. I pounded hard on the metal door. A man, young and attractive but disheveled and crazed, swung open the door as if he himself had also been drinking.

"I want to buy a Loch Ness Monster," I declared.

"Okay," he said, unimpressed with the four of us. "Come on in."

Inside we found an unmade bed with plaid flannel sheets, a hot plate, and a table cluttered with mounds of clay, googly eyes and hundreds of Loch Ness Monster figurines. I picked out one that was holding a little book and wearing a tiny pair of wire spectacles. It did, and still does, make me laugh to think of Nessie as bookish.

"So you live here?" I asked.

"Yep," he said, running a hand through his dirty hair. "I make and sell these to raise money for my research."

"Oh?" I said, intrigued there was a purpose to the kitsch. "What do you research?"

"The Loch Ness Monster," he said earnestly. "I'm trying to find her."

My friend snorted. "At a buck a piece, it's gonna take you forever."

"That may be true," he said, yawning as he scratched his beard. "But I'm crazy enough to wait."

Sweeping Down the Plain

L ast week, a crew from the city was patching some asphalt on our street when I came home from work. As I got out of my car, one of the crewmen approached me to ask if he could take a picture of the sycamore in our back yard.

The sycamore sits close to our house, just outside the living room window. Its trunk is so massive it would take three men standing around it touching fingertips to mimic its circumference. The tree is so tall it shoots out and over the top of our two-story home, nearly 50 feet above the tallest peak of the roof. The branches jut out in all directions, with limbs the size of most average trees, and the leaves that cloak it are larger than an adult face.

This tree was one of the major selling features of the home. When my husband and I first pulled up to the house and saw the massive tree brilliantly shading the sweet home below it, we gasped. "I know," our realtor beamed. "I know."

Having moved in just last spring, we've now officially seen the tree through every Oklahoma season. In the heat of the summer, we benefited greatly from the behemoth and all its widespread and lustrous foliage. The shade kept the back yard cool and our cooling bill low.

As we rolled into autumn, we were impressed, if not amused, at how many leaves fell from our great tree. Leaf after leaf after leaf piling up and blocking our front door, covering our driveway and clogging our gutters. The leaves became so overwhelming we had to call in professionals. When they pulled up, they burst out laughing at the foot-deep pile of face-sized leaves that covered every inch of our lawn. They worked for hours to gather, mulch and haul off the leaves. And not ten minutes after they had driven away, their trailer weighted down by our yard debris, another fresh blanket had fallen.

After a month or so, the leaves were all gone and we saw our beautiful sycamore naked for the first time. With the tree bare, its healthy, robust and gothic outline was breathtaking against the clear blue sky. When we endured our first snow and ice storm, we were awakened in the middle of the night by enormous, frozen branches snapping and hitting the roof.

Fast approaching our first official year in this home, we've watched the tree grow and change with the seasons. It has provided us shelter, shade, atmosphere and beauty. We've watched passersby stop in the middle of the street as their eyes search to find the top of the mammoth. We spend time each day picking up branches that have fallen or seeds that have gathered.

I'm enamored of our home and our neighbors. But the tree? The tree is overwhelming, high maintenance and intimidating. And of all things about our new place, it's my greatest point of pride.

But despite my pride and confidence in the gorgeous, giant creature that frames our home, I'm not without my doubts.

A few days ago, with my husband in Singapore on business, I was home alone with my two-and-a-half-year-old daughter in the middle of a windstorm.

I heard the wind begin to howl as I was making my way upstairs to bed. I turned on the TV to see if this was a storm that should have me fleeing to our basement for shelter. The meteorologist explained that it was an arctic blast moving down from the north and to expect violent and destructive winds until morning.

I heard a thump. I peered outside to see our trash can swirling around in the air, beating against the side of the house and slamming into the fence. I ran upstairs; the wind sounded as if it were getting stronger with every step I took. I threw open the curtains in my sleeping child's room to see trees in our neighbors' yard leaning over in the forceful winds. I looked up to see the sycamore branches reaching out over the roofline like giant skeleton hands. And in that moment, I was terrified of our big, beautiful tree.

Without hesitating, I reached for my child, ran down two flights of stairs and into our basement. Lowery curled up next to me— contouring herself around my pregnant belly—foggy with sleep. We lay together on the couch, wrapped tightly. I held her close, studying her beautiful sleeping face as I heard what sounded like more objects in our back yard being hoisted up and thrown about. I tried to decipher each noise. Glass breaking? Patio furniture catapulting? Shingles ripping from the roof? But as I lay there, embracing my precious child, I was only worried about one thing: our sycamore. I feared that it would be uprooted and would come crashing down on our house.

Never in my life, not ever so much as in that moment, did I feel more like a mother.

While I've read numerous articles on the care of sycamore trees, I don't turn to parenting books. I've become so beaten down by articles people write or links friends share that I've given up reading most everything on the topic.

I take such pride in my mighty child—her intellect, personality and twinkly eyes. For the most part, I've used her as the only yardstick to measure how good of a mother I am. She's incredibly bonded to me, loving, happy, healthy and smart. And so, rightly or wrongly, I've taken her thriving as a sign I must be doing something right.

But a couple of weeks ago a good friend of mine and I had a very intense debate about where we plan to send our children to school. The public/private school debate is as irritating and pointless as the breastfeeding/formula debate, but I've accepted that there's a debate at every stage.

My friend—whom I consider a wonderful mother—and I became entangled in a heated conversation about the benefits of private school versus public school, and her assertion that if she were to make the wrong choice in choosing a school, her children would suffer and forever be at a disadvantage.

I posited that, while choosing a school is an incredibly personal and difficult choice, it will not necessarily ruin a child's life or be anywhere near the only decision that will set them up for failure or success. And that while choosing a school is very important and I, too, struggle with the decision, I believe a child's education comes from many sources.

After our debate, I found myself upset for reasons I couldn't comprehend. She and I had engaged in lively debates a hundred times before without so much as a blink. After days of stewing over my unexplained emotions, I realized that what was bothering me was that I feared my friend didn't think I was a good mother.

Perhaps she took my more relaxed approach to choosing a school as a sign I wasn't invested in my child's future. Or that the choice I was planning to make (public) wasn't a good one, as it wasn't sacrificing enough (financially) to ensure my child's success.

More specifically, I was upset that she, or any of my friends, would measure my ability as a mother only by the choices I make among those polarizing options in parenting. For all the kind things said among friends, rarely is there praise for each other's parenting. And for the first time, despite the confidence I've always had in myself, and my parenting, I felt the winds of doubt blowing through the cracks.

But amidst the sounds of angry wind, as I lay there trembling in fear, with my child tucked safely under my arm, mentally going over every possible scenario of the storm, I had a revelation about motherhood. As if being without my husband, and being pregnant and consumed with fear, led me to realize how strong and capable and competent I am. Because in that moment, I wasn't making a decision from a two-sided choice. I wasn't worried about what others thought. I was simply in the moment with my child, and grateful for it. And finally fully aware that the only person who could judge if I was a good mother, was my child.

And she was snuggled close to me for strength and comfort.

The next morning we crawled out of our basement and opened the front door to assess the damage. I was surprised to find that everything was in its place, with the exception of the trash can, which had landed in the far corner of the yard. The patio furniture had barely moved. I must have imagined the sound of glass breaking. Only a handful of broken limbs littered our yard.

And as I stepped outside and peered up at the sycamore towering above our house, I was relieved to see it was still standing, as tall and strong as ever.

Having defiantly survived the storm.

Evaluations

I was told once that I don't handle criticism well.

And it really hurt my feelings.

Growing up, my favorite TV show was *Dr. Katz, Professional Therapist,* an animated series on Comedy Central in the late 90s. Come to think of it, I might have been a weird kid.

On the show, comedian Jonathan Katz voiced the therapist, while a variety of comedians' stand-up routines were repurposed as the ramblings of his patients. While it was by no means my first introduction to comedy, it did efficiently expose me to many of the most famous modern comedians. From that point on, I became obsessed with the profession.

What other profession demands high-energy performance, prompts brutal self-reflection, and allows hoards of people to anonymously judge one's professional ability on an extremely routine basis?

None that I can think of.

Except being a professor.

I've never done stand up in a dark nightclub for a crowd of drunks. But I regularly stand in front of a room full of people and try to get, and keep, their attention.

For both the instructor and the comedian, the goal is to appeal to the greatest number of people in the audience. Both have to entertain, challenge and inform. Both try not to alienate anyone. And both have to keep the audiences coming back. The comedian, to pay the bills; the instructor, to prepare them for the midterm.

But perhaps the biggest similarity between the comedian and the professor is the extreme way in which the professional is scrutinized.

Scrutiny that is both immediate and delayed. Both helpful and hurtful. External and internal.

As the comedian stands in front of the silent crowd, he can immediately tell he's bombing. Days later, he can read the critique in a critic's belabored review.

Every semester, a few weeks before final exams, college students get to evaluate their professors. They answer a series of questions in which they rank each professor on teaching style, course content, personality and grading fairness. There is also a comments section in which they can write any amount of feedback they feel necessary.

Student evaluations can be a wonderful thing. They give students a great amount of voice and power over an experience for which they are paying. Professors can use this feedback to improve their courses. And the university can judge the effectiveness of the professors it employs.

On top of student evaluations, professors undergo peer evaluations, in which a fellow professor sits in on a colleague's class to observe the teaching style. And finally, professors submit numerous documents, including their student and peer evaluations, for an annual performance review.

This semester, every class period was an immediate critique of my craft. Like the comedian, I have to read the room. Some days, I walked out of class after dramatically dropping the mic, with the glint of sweat on my brow and the sound of uproarious applause following me out the door. Other days, I ended class curled up under the lectern while students lined up to have me clarify every single thing I had said over the past hour.

And when student evaluations come in, which they do a week or so after the semester has ended, there is the long-form critique of everything I did or said or implied during the past semester.

This semester, by all accounts, was a good one. I taught more classes, and had more students, than I ever have in all my years of teaching. I stuck to my promise of replying to student emails the day I received them. I worked tirelessly on lecture notes and classroom activities. I returned all graded assignments within two weeks, and I memorized and used everyone's names.

The last day of the semester I drove home feeling as if I had given my all and truly felt there wasn't anything I would have done differently.

And yet, a week later, when the evaluations came in, my stomach tightened.

The report generates a numerical value to show how I performed in all the areas evaluated. It also shows me how my score compared to other faculty members. The cold hard data is easy to assess and accept.

But then there is the comments section.

That's where the nuances of both the professional and the critic are exposed. And more difficult to process.

I opened the comments section to find a screen full of dense text. My eyes skimmed furiously to see negative phrasing, criticism, judgment and disdain.

I quickly closed the document and sat very still at my desk. No matter how many students offered me good feedback throughout the semester, I can't help but view the end of term evaluations as the final word.

Looking at the life of a comedian, I know this feeling is common. Watching Louie C.K. in *Louie* tackle his own insecurities as others rub his face in them. Seeing how Amy Schumer joins in society's slam on her weight. Even those who are deeply self-aware are still hurt by hearing what they already know. So as I opened the comments section of my evaluations, I knew there would be no surprises. The good. The bad. I knew it all.

Fortunately, most every comment was positive, complimentary and gracious.

But then came those that weren't so glowing. Comments that demanded faster turnaround time on grades. That desired a harder midterm exam. That wanted longer lectures. That needed me to talk slower. Talk louder. Talk softer. Talk less. Provide more PowerPoints, provide fewer PowerPoints, help explain what a PowerPoint is. Grade tougher. Grade easier. Stop assigning grades.

If a student ever called me a racist—or heaven forbid, *boring*—I'd brush it off as radically unfounded. But when a student remarks that I'm not a strong lecturer, or I don't explain certain things thoroughly, or that I'm sometimes forgetful or disorganized, or points out a part of my personality for which I already feel insecure, it hurts down deep.

I prefer to walk around thinking my flaws, my weaknesses, my insecurities, are hidden well beneath my Spanx. And are my little secrets. So when they are all pointed out to me by others, who can see them so clearly, I feel vulnerable and exposed.

Because I'd rather not have my weaknesses confirmed. It removes the small glimmer of hope that they really don't exist.

And yet, if I had to evaluate them, the students whose approval I'm vying for, I wouldn't have the nicest things to say about everyone. Like the student who was always trying to push back paper deadlines. Or the student who always tried to outsmart me. The student who never showed up. The student who never gave any effort.

It's like the guy I dated in college. For years I wondered—and never knew—what he felt about me. And only later, with too many years invested, did I stop to look at what I truly felt about him.

It was mostly negative feedback.

From the array of fantastic shows about the life of a comedian, lately I'm drawn to *Comedians in Cars Getting Coffee*. Just like *Dr. Katz*, Jerry Seinfeld offers his audience exposure to numerous comedians and insight into their insecurities.

Seinfeld begins every show modeling a classic car he's picked out to represent the comedian he's about to pick up for a coffee date. He provides an in-depth description and visual inventory of a cool vintage automobile, while offering a candid and poetic reason behind its metaphorical representation of his comedic colleague.

Numerous cameras harnessed in the car allow viewers to witness a very genuine conversation between two professionals in the same field, as they make their way to a coffee shop. The comedians discuss various topics, like child rearing and life on the road. And intercut with beautiful footage of foaming milk and coffee pouring in slow motion, they talk about their lives in the field of comedy.

In nearly every episode of *Comedians in Cars,* the guest will admit to having bombed in front of an audience when just starting out in the profession. They talk of the frustration and the heartbreak of not getting laughs in the early years.

It's the equivalent of adjunct teaching.

They talk of the constant feedback from the audience. The absurd need to please the crowd, and the humility—and resentment—that comes with that.

And yet the comedian and the professor are also the kind of professionals who can't seem to find their place in any other line of work.

The constant performer.

Which makes me wonder if, perhaps, both sought out a profession that continually puts them in a position to be judged.

Is there some need they both have to be constantly evaluated, and to therefore be constantly evaluating themselves? While I'm not entirely sure how the comedian would respond, I imagine he or she would say exactly what I would:

No comment.

Muscle Memory

At my most recent OBGYN appointment, I told my doctor I was pretty certain I was suffering from BCS. He looked at me quizzically. "You know," I continued, "Broken Crotch Syndrome." His brow furrowed. I wondered if I had embarrassed him by exposing a gap in his medical knowledge. Then he smiled and said, "Ah, pain in your pelvis?"

I nodded.

When he asked me to explain the discomfort, I told him, first, to not use the word "discomfort" and second, to understand that the pain oscillated between sharp and intense to dull and throbbing. I was pretty sure the damn thing was broken.

"Totally normal," he said with a swat of the hand. "And I assure you, it isn't broken."

I sighed heavily, clearly not satisfied with his explanation for why walking up stairs felt like being hit repeatedly in my lady parts with a bag of hot nickels.

"Your body has been through this before," he tried explaining further. "So it's preparing itself."

I stared at him blankly.

"It's a simple case of muscle memory," he declared with finality.

I suppose my doctor might have a point. My body has been through a pregnancy once before. And a birth. And I know that muscles do, in fact, retain memory of processes or activities they have experienced before. My pelvis was remembering, perhaps quite vividly, how lengthy and difficult of a labor and delivery it was put through. And so, in the interest of self-preservation, my pelvis was holding up her hands like a stranger was pointing a gun.

Though my pelvis was remembering everything about the birthing process, fortunately my *mind* was only recalling certain aspects of it. Like all good defense mechanisms available to humans, the ability to erase traumatic experiences, sad moments or truly painful episodes from one's memory is the strongest.

Medical research tells us that physical pain has no memory. I remember the birth of my first child as one of the more painful experiences of my life. But I can't exactly recall the *feeling* of it. And so, when women get past the trauma of childbirth (and new motherhood), they actually, over time, forget the pain of it all. This is the only reason siblings exist.

But then, memory can work overtime to hold on to other aspects of our lives. Even if the memory is retained for the wrong reason.

One of my most vivid memories from childhood was watching the wedding of Princess Diana and Prince Charles, in the early hours of the morning, while vacationing with my family. I remember sitting on the soft green carpet in front of the television in our hotel room while my mother sat on the edge of one of the beds, daubing her eyes with tissues. My sister and brother played cards at the small table in the room, and my father slept soundly in the other bed. I remember the intricate details of Diana's wedding dress. I remember the floral pattern on the bedspreads. I remember the soft rumble of my father's snore.

Only when I was much older did I discover that Diana's wedding to Charles happened two years before I was born.

Psychologists call this "confabulation," or "false memories." I created and solidified an extremely strong memory in my mind simply by hearing the regular retelling of a family story that took place before my birth.

My fondest and strongest memories from childhood—ones not blocked from trauma, or fabricated from proximity—are connected to my unique and beautiful friendship with my best friend, Kate.

Having met at the age of three—when most experts agree we begin to retain memories—she plays a role in most every major memory from my childhood.

My strongest memory is a relationship.

If you ask my husband what his strongest memories from childhood are, he will say books. Specifically, comic books. When he was very young, his mother bought him a stack of comic books as a way to get him interested in reading. Her trick worked so well that Jim was able to read before kindergarten and is, to this day, intensely drawn to comic book mythology.

By realizing the pivotal aspects of our childhood memories, my husband and I can easily see how our minds function differently from each other in adulthood. I can recall specifics of moments dating back to three years of age. I never forget a face. Or a piece of clothing. Or a phrase that was spoken to me years ago. I remember how people stood when they told me a story. I recall eye color. Gestures. Emotions. I remember conversations. Facial features. Voices. Hands.

It is so powerful that the moment an unknown actor appears on screen, I can instantly remember a different color shirt the actor was wearing in a different role, think back to what he was saying in that other role, and let my mind work around the memory until I declare that he was the guy in the cat food commercial six years ago.

But my memory stops at the written word. I can read something over and over and over and it's like an egg on Teflon. *The Great Gatsby* is one of my favorite books, but I have to reread it frequently, and when I do, I'm shocked when Myrtle Wilson is run over by the car. Every single time.

Jim, on the other hand, can remember every word he's ever read. If his eyes skimmed it once, it's in his head forever. Not only can he remember what he's read, but what year he read it, and in which periodical. This is why he was extremely successful in school and college and scored almost perfect on the SATs and the GRE. His vocabulary is endless. His grasp of the complexities of the Middle East and all the leaders' names (spelled correctly) is astonishing. If he read it in a newspaper, magazine or textbook, it's his for life.

But his total recall stops at details surrounding personal interactions. He struggles to remember specifics of conversations. The number of times I've verbally told him an important piece of information, only to have him ask for the details again the next day, are countless. But I'd never call him forgetful. Besides, if I really want him to remember something, I know to just send him an email.

Between our two memories, Jim's is seemingly more useful. He gets more conventional recognition out of retaining facts, words, dates, and events than I get out of recalling feelings, emotions, experiences and faces. But when we allow our memories to work together, we can fully round out an experience.

A few months back, at my husband's company Christmas party, we walked into the room to find a crowd of his coworkers and their spouses. I immediately recognized every single person and was able to call them all by name and ask them how they were feeling about their child's upcoming milestone, the milestone they had spoken of with such vivid emotion last Christmas. And when a coworker brought up the previous night's football game, my husband jumped in with all the backlogged statistics he had read.

It's not quite *A Beautiful Mind*, or accurately counting toothpicks, but it is the summation of our relationship.

So as we are fast approaching the birth of our second child, we find our muscles remembering vastly different moments from the same experience. As usual, my memory is completely physical, experiential and emotional. My body is reacting strongly to its own memory. My pelvis is assuming the position. My heart is pulsing with excitement. My gut is tightening with fear.

Jim is focused on the specifics. He's recounting all the pamphlets he had read in the hospital. He's recalling the details of how we check in at Labor and Delivery. He's remembering how many doses of pain medicines were most effective during my recovery.

And when I see how our memories retain different aspects of the same experience, I realize how much our memories are different simply because we observe life in different ways. Jim has always been drawn to details, complexities, specifics. I've always been drawn to emotions, conversations, intentions. And so perhaps it's natural for people to retain only those aspects of life that entice them the most.

Which is why I've enjoyed this portion of our marriage, the portion with children, more than any other time in our relationship. Because never before have we both been so incredibly enticed by the same thing.

Even if we remember each moment in different ways.

I can recall and mimic the exact octave of our child's most joyous laugh. I can accurately draw her birthmark from memory. I remember the feel of her skin at birth.

Jim can recall every daily take home sheet that recounted what she did and ate at school on a specific day. He knows every book he's ever read to her by heart. He remembers what she weighed at every doctor's visit in the first year.

And we try to concentrate on these memories. Because my hammer-pelted crotch is reminding me of all the painful memories we also have with our child. Memories at which we both still wince. The pain. The exhaustion. The screaming cries of our child. Postpartum depression. Ear infections. Shots. Grieving the loss of our childless lives.

But memory is the mirror of life. It reflects the good with the bad.

And our life changes every day. Every day is a new memory, and soon, we will have another child to fill our minds with even more. So as life races on, my husband and I have promised to put our heads together.

So we won't forget to remember it all.

For Shame

I do not have a sense of smell.

I know, I know, your next question is inevitably: "Are you able to taste?" Or maybe you want to ask: "Are your other senses heightened?" Or perhaps you are the kind who can't help but inquire: "So, you wouldn't know if I farted?"

In answer to the litany of questions I get about my condition, I can tell you this: Yes, I can taste. I still have a fairly refined palate; I can distinguish between white and red wine by sight and taste alone. No, my other senses aren't heightened; my nightstand is littered with dried-up contact lenses. And, just to humor you, you sick bastard, I would still know if you farted; my ears work fine.

I discovered I had no sense of smell when I was 10 years old watching a television commercial for nasal spray. A man with a microphone was blindfolding people on the street and holding various fruits under their noses to show them that their nasal passages were too clogged to enjoy the most basic smells in life. I watched as one woman blindly smelled an orange, to which she noted she couldn't detect a scent. I laughed and thought: *Well, yeah, because oranges don't have a scent.*

There are moments when I feel a sensation that I liken to smell, such as when I chew the kind of gum that looks like a Chiclet and comes in blister packs of nine. Or when it's muggy outside and I mistake the dampness hitting my nostrils for a foul odor. And a few times, and only while I was pregnant, I could smell the gasoline at the pump.

There aren't any true concerns or limitations. No doctor has found the condition alarming, or even all that interesting. One down side is that it's not uncommon for a child of mine to be sitting in her own feces for a tad longer than is recommended by pediatricians. But it's only because if I don't hear a wet fart, or see it creeping out the diaper and up her back, I don't have much to go on.

The most annoying aspect of my condition, however, is that I walk around in life always a little worried that I might unknowingly stink. I practice a fairly rigorous personal hygiene routine. I keep the house clean. I don't eat onions. I compulsively purchase mints, gum, perfumes, Febreze, scented lotions and fragrance candles. I'm not sure I've ever purchased an item that was "unscented." And I haven't farted in 20 years.

The fear is just too deep.

But I think it's normal to be a little insecure about a personal deficiency.

In every course I've ever taught—in the field of political science— I've devoted a block of time each class period to discuss current events. In the beginning, I did this simply because I wholly believe in the benefit of civil discourse and the power of an informed citizenry.

For the most part, functioning adults can peacefully disagree on an issue and respectfully discuss it far better than is perhaps assumed. Colleagues often ask me if the debates ever escalate to a troubling degree. Or if the conservatives yell and throw things while the liberals huddle together and cry.

There have only been a few times a student became emotional— one even walked out of class—but on the whole, people are respectful and mature. In fact, in all my years of teaching, the issue that most often arises is not across party lines. The biggest issue, in fact, is something I refer to as Awareness Shaming.

This happens when a person shames another for not knowing something, typically—though not limited to—a news story.

One person brings up a topic: "Did you hear about the bombings in Whatsitsnameistan?"

Another person says: "No, I haven't."

And the first person responds with something like: "Do you live under a rock!?" Then continues the shaming further by expressing extreme shock and disgust with dramatic body language and theatrical phrases like, "I just can't believe you haven't heard about that! What do you do all day!?"

I once thought Awareness Shaming only occurred in the classroom. That was certainly where I saw it happen on a daily basis. But Awareness Shaming is just as common in everyday life. And I've estimated it affects nearly one in two Americans per day. So, in all likelihood, you just finished shaming the person next to you, or they are currently shaming you.

Given what I do for a living, there is a significant expectation for me to know any and all things related to politics, both in the United States and around the world. But if you quiz me on, say, the latest poll data on the gubernatorial race in Maryland, I'm more than likely going to let you down. Though my research is in a specialized portion of Political Science—public administration, which studies bureaucracy and nonprofits—as a member of the field I try my level best to stay current on the political climate.

Which changes hourly.

I often wonder if I would have faired better in a discipline like History or Philosophy. All the important events have already happened, and the great minds are already dead.

I'll be the first to admit that I fall short of staying up-to-date on every single shooting, bombing, bill, hearing, debate, election, famine and indictment. I often feel overwhelmed and burdened by how much there is to know. And how many outlets there are to know it from. But still, I try. I read the paper. My phone buzzes as often with news updates as it does with text messages. And given how much my mother texts, this is saying something. I tune in to NPR every time I'm in the car. Which means I'm getting the first half of a really great story about a rice farmer in the middle of a war zone, or the last half of a segment on our sanctions against Iran. I'm on daily email lists for publications put out from Capitol Hill, policy institutes, and the foreign press.

But despite my best efforts, I often find myself in the middle of a party, or at lunch with my sister, or in front of a class full of eager students, admitting that I have not heard of the event about which they are speaking.

And while I'm certainly not *ashamed*, I am often shamed.

Sometimes it isn't even about high brow political jargon. Sometimes it's a simple "How have you never heard of the band Spoon?!" And heaven forbid I admit that I have no fucking clue how to sync my phone calendar to the one on my computer.

Knowledge is power. But it shouldn't be a weapon.

I value staying current with events from here and around the world. And I appreciate the opportunity to be educated on an issue from someone who has more knowledge on the subject than I. But the way in which people tend to react when you admit you don't know a story, an event, a person, a band, or a keyboard shortcut on your Mac is not doing much to propel people forward. When I get Awareness Shamed, I feel talked down to. I feel beaten up. I feel as vulnerable as when an acquaintance tells me she saw me "out and about the other day" and all I can think was that it was probably the exact moment I was dislodging a wedgie.

So I tell my students that in our debates they are not allowed to Awareness Shame. If a classmate hasn't heard about a certain event, don't shame or poke fun. Instead, I ask them to use their reaction to educate, not denigrate.

And since making this a class rule, I've noticed students are much more likely to participate in the discussion.

Gaps in knowledge are about the same as walking around with a sensory limitation; you'd be surprised how well you can still function.

Smells don't interest me because they aren't part of my daily life. But there are a lot of sights, sounds, tastes and touches I love and explore fully.

In the meantime, I rely on my husband to alert me to poopy diapers, the smell of smoke and soured milk. And, in turn, I occasionally offer to change the dirty diapers, promise to grab our photos if there's a fire, and agree to pick up milk on the way home from work.

There is no shame in not knowing something. Not being good at something. Not having a sense of smell. The only shame is not *pursuing* knowledge. Not *trying* to be good at something. Not having a sense of self.

So I find it paramount that the benefit of the doubt be given first, and let the shaming be reserved for when a dog shits in your shoe.

Because even I know, that stinks.

Gesundheit

My pregnancy with you,
I was able to conceive with ease.
And somehow this convinced me,
These nine months would be a breeze.

Because with my first pregnancy,
I threw up daily all around.
But it was a flawless gestation;
Not one issue could be found.

But *your* pregnancy I've felt so great,
I was practically ecstatic.
Until a series of incidents,
Showed things were problematic.

The first problem they detected,
Was possible Down Syndrome.
The doctor called to tell me the results,
And left me to panic alone.

But further intense testing,
And researching to frustration,
Revealed that all the needless worry,
Was over a simple miscalculation.

Then my right leg began to swell,
And the doctor thought it possible,
That I had formed a blood clot,
And he sent me to the hospital.

Naked I lay while they scanned my body,
To find my veins and arteries unscathed.
To which I breathed a sigh of relief,
And promised next time I would shave.

Then came the issue of sugar,
Which polluted my urine like debris.
I shrugged and told the doctor,
That maybe I just have sweet pee.

Despite my sound argument,
My doctor demanded with insistence,
That I go straight down to the lab,
And be tested for insulin resistance.

So every week I'd fast at night,
And go to the lab in the early morn.
But all those glucose readings,
Showed my blood sugar was in the norm.

Then I developed a month long cold,
And my begging was quixotic.
Because the doctor finally caved,
And prescribed a strong antibiotic.

For 10 solid days I took those pills,
But women, you know the next section.
Pregnancy plus antibiotic,
Equals a raging yeast infection.

So 10 more days on different meds,
And I was finally feeling restored.
With no pregnancy problems,
I was even getting a little bored.

But at 32 weeks and still sugary pee,
My doctor, who's much like Archimedes,
Demanded I do one more test,
By which they diagnosed diabetes.

So that means four times a day,
I have to prick my finger.
In the morning and after meals,
To see how long the glucose will linger.

I have to cut out all sugar,
And plan my meals to a science.
Plus send my doctor a weekly report,
To prove my strict compliance.

And though my diet and exercise
Were a true marvel of discipline,
A few weeks after my diagnosis,
I was prescribed insulin.

So between the shots in the belly,
And all the finger pricking from dawn,
If I drink a glass of water,
I can easily sprinkle our lawn.

Then about two weeks ago,
At a routine doctor's exam.
My amniotic fluid looked way too low,
When they reviewed the sonogram.

The sudden drop in fluid,
Caused my doctor a lot of stress.
So I was immediately sent home,
And put on strict bed rest.

Which means I can only get up,
To shower or to pee.
So I just lie around and fan myself,
Like a member of the bourgeois.

Now when the boredom and loneliness,
Become too great to handle,
I make myself a cup of tea,
And stream another *Scandal.*

And twice a week we review the evidence,
Hoping to be acquitted.
As my doctor gives me a thorough exam,
To see if I need to be admitted.

But so far all the ultrasounds,
And every urine sample,
Say you and I are doing fine,
Though our fluids aren't quite ample.

So they can poke and prod me,
And you can bounce on my bladder.
And they can keep me in a state of worry,
But it truly doesn't matter.

For here's the deal my darling child,
None of this is a bother.
There's simply no lengths that I won't go,
For you, your sister or your father.

Because I know, despite what I'm told
In the medical vernacular,
There is no doubt in my racing mind,
That you are anything but spectacular.

And though it's been a long road,
I can't wait for our first embrace.
And every moment will be worth it,
When I see your perfect face.

But now I have a simple request;
I hope you will abide.
When I go into labor,
Let's aim for a sneeze and slide.

Overlay

D espite being the more grounded of the two of us, my husband is quite the optimist.

When he's not being a realist or a pessimist.

When we first started dating, Jim planned a romantic evening out for us. This included seeing the new exhibition at a museum, drinks at my favorite bar, and dinner at a restaurant I had promised myself I'd never patronize again. While Jim's default is to always let me have my way, that night he refused. He drove us to the restaurant with me protesting the entire way. When we pulled into the lot, he put the car in park, shut off the engine, turned to me and said, "I'm about to give you an overlay experience."

I blushed at his forwardness, but he then explained what he meant by "overlay." He believed that all bad experiences can be redone, with the hopes of having a better experience the second time. So by taking me to a restaurant in which I'd had a bad experience, he was determined to overlay it with a good one.

And it worked.

We had such a fantastic date that night, the restaurant is now one of our favorite spots.

While this seemed small, Jim's overlay idea became a substantial component of our relationship. We re-experienced numerous restaurants, various trips, and dozens of movies together. But it also became somewhat of a philosophy of our life together: no bad experience is the final word.

Sometimes the overlays were small: Jim re-watching *Annie Hall* with me and finally agreeing it had merit (he's still bitter it beat out *Star Wars* for Best Picture). And sometimes they were significant: the birth of our second child overlaying the experience of our first.

The experience birthing our first child was a bad one. Incredibly long labor, hours of pushing, extreme tearing (men, your life is a cake walk), excruciating PUPPS rash *after* delivery (Google image this, but not before dinner), no milk supply leading to my daughter's severe dehydration and readmission into the hospital, the horror of trying to defecate after a vaginal delivery (seriously, as a gender we need to talk about this more), and postpartum depression.

The gamut of horrible experiences.

But on the eve of our second daughter's birth, my husband assured me the experience would overlay the first. He even argued the more horrible the first experience, the greater the overlay.

And dammit if he wasn't right again.

I hardly even noticed I'd delivered London. Short labor, only a handful of pushes, no tearing, no rash, no dehydration issues, and I didn't even bat an eye taking a shit after birth. And, as far as I can tell, I've even escaped postpartum depression. I came home with a quiet, sweet, sleepy baby who politely existed in our lives the first few weeks as if she didn't want to bother anyone. This made me believe I was ready to take on one of life's greatest challenges:

The family vacation.

Because Memorial Day was upon us, we decided that an overnight stay somewhere close would be the perfect way to spend our first vacation as a family of four. We chose a town that was a two-hour drive from home. I found the perfect hotel that boasted a beautiful pool and its walking distance to family-friendly restaurants. I bought tickets to a science museum and the zoo, and I made sure the botanical gardens were open over the holiday break.

The night before we left, I packed more brilliantly than I'd ever packed before. I had a bag of snacks, snacks that were neither choking hazards nor produced crumbs. I had all the baby's gear— portable crib, stack of diapers, wad of burp cloths, onesies, blankets, swaddle sacks and lotion. I had all the toddler gear— books, dolls, underwear, clothes, eight pairs of shoes, a sun hat and detangler. I had swimsuits for all four of us. I had sunscreen. I had the double stroller. I had chargers for all electronic devices. I even had the fucking *Frozen* soundtrack.

The morning we were set to depart, Jim and I stopped for coffee and gas, and were thrilled with ourselves for getting on the road at the exact time for which we had aimed and synchronized our watches. During the drive to our destination, the uninterrupted conversation and peacefully sleeping children lured us both into a false sense of security.

We had a pleasant time when we stopped for lunch. And the first destination—the science museum—was a huge success. But before dinner, with everyone waiting in the hotel room while I fed the baby, things started to unravel. It began with a slight burning in my right eye. When I took my contacts out (and laid them on the nightstand) I felt no relief. My husband joked that I had pink eye. I laughed, until I looked over at Lowery and noticed her left eye was gunky. And pink. Luckily, my brilliant packing included every single medication in our bathroom, even a half empty bottle of antibiotic eye drops.

I'm not implying that trying to get eye drops into an uncooperative preschooler ruined the trip. But it sure worked up a nice sweat before dinner.

Once the baby was fed, and all infected eyes were treated, we decided to walk to a nearby restaurant. I had London strapped to my chest, and Lowery held my husband's hand as we strolled out of the hotel to discover it was sprinkling. Slightly.

As we walked, however, the slight sprinkle turned into a light rain. One block down. Then the light rain became an average rain, in which puddles start to form. Another half a block down. Then the rain started to pick up to the point my husband hoisted our child to his hip, ineffectively put his hand on top of her head to block the water, and started to run. Because I had an infant strapped to the front of me, and was wearing sandals with no tread, I slowed down and clutched the brick walls of the buildings we were passing. By the time we got to the restaurant door, rain was falling in a manner most often seen during hurricanes. Or movies about shipwrecks.

I'm not implying that getting drenched with rainwater on our walk to the restaurant ruined our trip. But it sure cooled us off from all the eye-drop wrestling.

When we were safely inside the restaurant, we were told there would be a thirty-minute wait for a table. This didn't worry me. In my brilliant packing I had managed to bring a small backpack filled with coloring books and stickers to occupy my three-year-old in such a situation. But after we had been waiting more than an hour, all the stickers were placed and all the pages were colored. When our name was finally called, we were taken back to a table surrounded by roughly 15 other empty tables. In fact, the restaurant was nearly vacant.

I'm not implying that waiting more than an hour for a table when there were clearly no other people occupying it ruined our trip. But it certainly allowed us time to work up an appetite.

Another hour passed before our meal was delivered. The waiter explained that the delay was because the restaurant was "slammed." The only bright spot of the three-hour meal was a balloon artist who came to our table as we were trying to pay the bill. Lowery asked for a bunny rabbit, which he quickly made to her extreme enjoyment. She was so excited, in fact, that she leapt out of her seat to come show me her new animal, tripped over the balloon artist's foot and collided with the concrete floor. She screamed a scream not normally possible from such small lungs. This awoke our infant, who promptly tried to rival her sister's volume. I scooped up my three-year-old and headed to the lobby with both children screaming uncontrollably. With no option, I sat down on the floor to feed the baby while using my one free arm to wipe the blood off of my other child's knees, all while my husband finished paying the bill.

The screaming from both children lasted the entire walk back to the hotel.

I'm not implying that the extremely awful restaurant experience ruined our trip. But I do think it was responsible for putting all four of us in a pretty foul mood.

Back in our hotel room and in dry clothes, Lowery was beginning to exhibit signs of mental instability. She pulled everything out of every bag, all the pillows off the bed and then ran to the bathroom and attempted to lock herself in. I tried to help my husband with her antics, but I was occupied by our inconsolable infant.

For over an hour I worked to calm my inexplicably crying baby, while my husband resorted to every disciplinary tactic ever invented to try to calm down our wound-up child. Lowery is strong-willed and independent. To that we are accustomed. But this night was like nothing we'd ever seen. She had gone full-on Linda Blair.

Meanwhile, our infant, who had barely uttered a peep in her first few weeks of life, was screaming as though she'd just realized she had exited the womb. At one point, the front desk called our room to raise concerns about the noise level. We could barely hear each other over the two screaming girls.

"I don't negotiate with terrorists!" my husband screamed at one point as our three-year-old attempted to stick her head through a coat hanger.

"When is your vasectomy scheduled?!" I yelled over the high-pitched screech of our infant.

Lowery, who had opened the two complimentary bottles of water and poured them in the toilet, fought our demands that she get on the bed and go to sleep. She cried and screamed and pouted and, to my complete horror, spit.

Watching my child—my sweet, typically well-behaved child—literally spit at us made something inside of me snap. And I yelled. I yelled louder than the screaming children. Louder than I'd ever yelled. And when I stopped, Lowery looked at me, completely unfazed by my outburst, and yelled back, "I'm just *not* tired!"

With that pronouncement, she threw herself dramatically on the bed. And as her head hit the pillow, even before the rest of her body had landed, she was completely asleep.

My husband and I looked at each other in shock, not even realizing that London had miraculously stopped crying as well and had passed out asleep in my arms. Jim tip toed over to Lowery's bed and covered her with a blanket. I laid the baby gently down in the crib. And we silently crawled into bed together, trembling while we held each other like Leo and Kate in the icy waters.

I'm not implying that our three-year-old ruined our family vacation, but she totally did.

The next morning, Lowery popped up looking refreshed and happy. She bounced over to our bed to give us kisses. We rose up like two hung over frat boys to kiss her back. We had taken the zoo trip away from her the night before as a failed attempt to negotiate, which left us with only one remaining activity. The activity that had most excited Lowery. The activity that was making her jump up and down on the bed, gleefully laughing. I handed her swimsuit to her and called down to the front desk to check the pool hours. It was only 6:00 a.m.

"Oh, I'm sorry to tell you this," said the receptionist. "The pool is currently closed."

"I figured it was too early," I replied. "But what time will it open?"

"You've misunderstood me. It's *closed*. For repairs."

To avoid another meltdown, we promised Lowery we would let her play in the sprinkler when we got back home. This pacified her, and she happily helped us pack. But when we got in the car, Jim and I both cursed under our breath to see the rain clouds ahead.

Ten minutes into our journey home, a mere 18 hours after the trip began, Lowery said she needed to use the bathroom. The last sign we passed said the next rest stop was 30 miles ahead. Lowery began to cry, yelling that she really needed to go and couldn't hold it.

Jim and I contemplated our options, which were to stuff all of London's diapers down Lowery's pants while going 80 miles per hour down the highway, or to pull off on the side of the road. Neither seemed advisable, so instead we sped, promising Lowery candy if she could hold it. (I wasn't going up for Mother of the Year this trip.)

When we finally made it to the rest stop, Lowery bounced out of the car and ran next to me holding her crotch. She perched herself on the toilet, but I heard nothing. Pure silence.

"I don't have to go any more," she smiled up at me.

Rather than leave her there on the toilet, get back in the car and drive away, I'll always praise myself for deciding to take her with us.

Back in the car and ten more minutes down the road, London began screaming. Loudly. We contemplated our options. Me crawling in the back seat while the car went 90 down the highway, or pulling off to the side of the road. Neither was advisable, so we drove another 20 solid minutes with our infant screaming in the dog octave.

When we finally stopped, I jumped in the back seat, and the moment I placed the pacifier in her mouth, before her lips could even seal around it, she fell asleep.

Back on the road again, Lowery softly said, "Okay, I really do have to go this time."

What seemed like hours later, we pulled into our driveway and sat there with the engine still running and rain beating down on the hood. Both children were finally sleeping in the back seat. After a few moments of silence, tears began rolling down my cheeks. When my gentle crying became audible sobbing, Jim turned to look at me.

At first his face was twisted with concern, but then it morphed into an enormous grin.

"Why are you smiling?" I said, as snot started to collect on my upper lip.

"Because," he said with a laugh, "just imagine the overlay."

Dressing on the Side

I first met Melissa at the open house for the day care center our children now attend together. At the time, the director of the school hosted a dinner for incoming parents to ease them through the tumultuous transition from maternity leave to full time childcare.

The event was arranged so parents could drop off their infants in one of the classrooms—where three of the school's teachers eagerly awaited—and then meander into the dining hall to meet other shell-shocked and sleep-deprived new parents.

Melissa and her husband showed up a little late. She had her newborn son, Jack, pressed tightly to her, nursing him. All the other parents—especially me—were ecstatic at the thought of free childcare for an hour, and we had happily dropped our babies and ran. But not Melissa. She had her son in her arms, looking lovingly down at him as he blinked up at her.

At the time, our babies were mere weeks old. I was in the darkest period of postpartum depression, having long given up the ability to nurse, and was still struggling wildly to bond with my child. Watching her effortlessly cuddle and nurse her baby—the only mother in the packed room to reject the available childcare—I decided definitively that I hated Melissa.

After that night I tried to avoid her. When I saw her in the halls during morning drop off, I cringed. She would so carefully and lovingly place her precious son in the teacher's arms, hand over a bucket of breast milk, and float effortlessly out of the room accompanied by blue birds and field mice.

I would awkwardly hand over my child, leave her portions of formula and slink out of the room, wondering if I should have held my kid longer or brought a warmer blanket.

Three years and two children later, mothering is now natural, fun, and fulfilling. But in the beginning, every aspect of it felt monumental, and I struggled to adapt. Especially the part in which I realized, for the first time, that I am susceptible to female competition.

This isn't to say I didn't have my fair share of this in junior high. But on the whole, being a female never registered as anything other than the occasional pap smear and picking a brand of tampons. When I became a mother, however, my eyes were opened to the two greatest downfalls of our sex: intra-gender competition, and salads as a meal.

Oddly, these two aren't unrelated.

In fact, most women suffer from both of these in a chicken-or-the-egg fashion. Although I assume competition came first because I think it is somehow hard-wired into women.

Eating rabbit food, however, is a learned behavior.

I'll never fully understand why women compete with each other so much. I truly believe we don't intend to. We don't mean to approach other women as competitors, and I'd like to think we don't view womanhood as a competition. But I'm seeing less and less evidence to the contrary.

When I first met Melissa, I didn't stop to think that perhaps she just had a different way of coping with her struggles as a new mom (which I found out years later was true). Or, that perhaps the only reason she was holding her son that night was because they came late and didn't know childcare was available (I found out later this was also true). Or that maybe, just *maybe,* I intimidated her as well (also, true).

Instead, I saw her as an opponent.

I looked at her and assumed that what I was witnessing was a woman being *better* than I was. Handling motherhood better. Bonding to her child quicker. Balancing work more easily. Losing the pregnancy weight faster.

Which leads me to the other aspect of womanhood I'm exhausted by: salads as a meal. When did this become standard practice for women? I'm not saying a salad with a whole chicken breast on it mixed with avocados, cheese, eggs and tortilla chips smothered in twelve ounces of ranch dressing can't be a meal. But ordering a small side salad—without croutons and with the dressing on the side—and telling me that "it just sounds good" is the practice of the clinically insane. Or a crazy ritual of competitors. Mind games. Trash talk.

The only thing worse than watching a beautiful, brilliant friend pick at a small plate of grass is hearing the abuse she throws on herself while she does it. Claiming she needed to eat a salad for lunch because she "had a carby breakfast" or because she's "been so bad lately."

Now, I have no issues with wanting to be healthy. I make—for the most part—healthy choices in my day-to-day life. I cook myself a healthy and intricate breakfast every morning. I cook most nights of the week. I frequently purchase almonds, and make substantial efforts to eat them. I drink about 90 ounces of water a day. I can't tell you the last time I had a candy bar. And, given enough nacho cheese sauce, I can really wolf down some vegetables.

My issue is how women punish themselves for every crumb that hits their lips. Or the sweeping declarations they make, like if they eat carbs they just "balloon up." Or the bold lifestyle choices they constantly take on, like giving up sugar or only eating "clean." And what the hell is with all the juice cleanses? Here, take this spinach, mush it up, drink it, and shit constantly for a week solid. You'll feel amazing!

I can't help but think the only reason any woman would subject herself to that is because she's trying to achieve a standard put on her by someone else. To become a worthy opponent. They see a healthier, skinnier, firmer woman and go into juice-cleanse, shitting-round-the-clock, salad-as-a-meal, hyper-competitive mode.

So then there's a beautiful, talented, brilliant woman who spends way too much time obsessing over food and weight and gluten. Using food as a punishment. Self-loathing. Feeling guilt while eating.

And nothing ruins a good steak like tears.

Now, again, making good choices is fine. Drinking water instead of Coke. Fruit as a side. Less red meat. Move your body more. Many, many people do this without even giving it a thought, or attaching it to a childhood memory, or posting about it on Facebook.

These people are called men.

Men don't sit around picking shamefully at their food. Nor do they sit around comparing themselves to other men. My husband has never once looked at another man and said, "Do you think he's a better father than I am?" Nor has he taken so much as a breath while inhaling bacon.

Without constantly being threatened by each other, and without giving a thought to eating sugar or enjoying a stiff drink, men have all the time in the world to walk around inventing shit and getting paid twice as much for it.

And sure, I'm fully aware of the pressures on females to have it all—ambition, small waists, high powered jobs, vulnerability, high sex drive, nurturing demeanor, flawless skin, white teeth, perky breasts and leadership skills.

But maybe, just *maybe*, if we women all started acting like that pressure wasn't there, it might one day disappear. If we started looking at each other as teammates before opponents, then we could stop all the competition and take each other out for lunch.

And order a hamburger.

We would stop picking at our food. We would stop comparing ourselves to other women. We would stop thinking that spin class is the only reason we're allowed to eat a bite of cake. And we could put our energy more on taking down the man.

We can start by eating some fries off his plate.

I speak from experience. Three years since that first dinner where I met Melissa, she and I have become close friends. It started because our children are friends. Her son Jack and my daughter Lowery adore each other. In a beautiful, simple way that children can before the expectations of society are thrust upon them.

And when Melissa and I became pregnant at the same time with our second children, a deeper bond was formed. Text messages, emails and meals together helped us move past the competition and into a place that felt nurturing and comfortable.

When our daughters were born, we celebrated their health and were grateful for our own body's ability to carry them. We don't talk about breastfeeding or parenting philosophies or losing baby weight. And when we want to share a meal, we don't raise the stakes by ordering a salad.

Now, my youngest daughter London, and Melissa's daughter Katy, are in day care class together. On London's first day, I was hysterical. At work, I sat at my desk crying, scrolling through the pictures of her birth while R.E.M. played in the background. Then my phone lit up with a text from Melissa. It was a picture she had snapped of our two daughters. During drop off, she had laid Katy down beside London on the big mat in the classroom. As if instinctively, the girls extended their arms and grasped each other's hands. It was only for a moment, Melissa explained, but it was a palpable love between two female friends.

So perhaps the next generation of women won't have this cyclical problem of eating to compete with one another. Maybe the women of the next generation will have it all figured out. Will spend time talking about improving lives and changing the world and saving the planet. And they won't get hung up on the next diet or exercise fad or boasting about their parenting philosophies all over social media.

Maybe the women of the next generation will just be who they are. And proud of it. And will figure out early on that they are equal to the opposite gender, the way Lowery and Jack did. And maybe they will figure out early on that they are equal to each other, like London and Katy have.

They won't compete. And they will eat.

This is the hope I have for the next generation of women. Because this is the generation of women I'm helping to raise. And here's my driving thought every day as I do: I peek into the future, twenty years down the road, and I see my two daughters at lunch together. They meet regularly because they are close, best friends even. There is no competition between them. Just love and support. It catches my breath how beautiful and strong they've become. They are laughing while they eat their sandwiches. And while I can't quite make out what they are saying, I'm hoping only one thing for my beautiful girls:

They are talking about something of substance.

But not of weight.

Rise and Shine

I am a morning person.

My husband might protest this statement, but it is a fact that I love the mornings. I might look like death lying next to him when the alarm starts blaring, I might swat him away as he tries to wake me, and I might threaten to divorce him if he doesn't turn the lights back off. But that doesn't mean I'm not a morning person.

As a child, I always awoke extremely early. My siblings were asleep, my mother was asleep, even the farm animals that surrounded our country home were asleep. But I sprang out of bed impossibly early and bounced into the kitchen where I would always find my father blowing on a steaming cup of black coffee.

During my infancy, while I was still in a carrier car seat, my father would bundle me up and take me to the donut shop on Saturday mornings. He would set the car seat on a table and allow the elderly regulars to fuss over me while he purchased a few donuts and a smoldering cup of coffee. He would sit and eat, talking to me as I blinked back at him from behind the five-point harness.

Later, as a toddler, my father would watch *Garfield and Friends* with me on Saturday mornings while I ate my cereal. He would sit beside me on the couch, reading the paper and cautiously sipping on a piping hot cup of coffee.

When I was a little older, perhaps 10, my father thought it was time for me to grow up. And all grown ups burn their tender tongues each morning on a scalding cup of coffee.

I was reluctant at first. But my father had a plan to make me his coffee companion. He would set out two coffee mugs. Fill one to the brim with boiling, black liquid. In the other cup, he would put a splash of coffee, perhaps no more than a tablespoon, and fill the rest with milk. And there we sat, my father and I, hours before the rest of our family awoke, sharing a pot of coffee. Over time, the ratio of coffee to milk in my cup slowly started to even. By the time I was 14, I was drinking a full cup of straight, black coffee every morning.

And it's been that way ever since.

Our mornings together weren't just relegated to donuts, cartoons and coffee on Saturdays. My father was up with me every morning during the week. He made my breakfast, took me to school and made sure I got the day started off right.

Though we lived on several acres of sprawling land, our tiny house didn't have a garage, so our cars were subjected to the brutality of Oklahoma weather. Sometimes, even in the early mornings, the car was hot and muggy and we sweated all the way to school. Other times, the car was the perfect temperature and we were able to ride to school with the windows down and The Commitments' rendition of *Mustang Sally* blasting. But typically, and it sure *seemed* like every single morning, my father's vehicle was covered in a sheet of ice.

On mornings like that, we would get in the car, and my dad would start the engine and sit patiently waiting for the vents to spit out even a tiny breath of heat. Once we felt a puff of heat he would put the car in reverse. Despite the fact that the entire Jeep was completely covered in a thick layer of opaque ice, he'd blindly back the car out anyway.

"We have to face East," he'd say.

And I'd nod knowingly through the sound of my chattering teeth. He'd carefully turn the car completely around, until we were facing East, and then put the car in park.

"You tell me when," he'd say, patiently sitting there, unscrewing the lid to his thermos of bubbling coffee. And I would do what I did every freezing, school-day morning: I'd stare at the windshield, waiting for it to glisten.

After a few minutes of watching a layer of ice an inch thick stay completely frozen, I'd instruct my father to get closer to the sun. He'd put his thermos in the cup holder, throw the car in drive, and inch down our half-mile, dirt road driveway. When we would slowly creep into a part of the driveway where the sun was able to break through the trees and slightly brighten the thick layer of ice in front of us, I'd yell, "Stop! Right here!"

If we waited long enough, if we possessed just the right amount of patience—much like the patience it took my father over the years to reduce my milk intake and increase my coffee consumption—we could see the windshield start to glisten.

It would sparkle, just slightly, down near the wipers. Amateurs would take this as a sign it was time to turn the wipers on. But my father and I had become seasoned professionals. Eventually, the glistening would get brighter and wider, like a plate of diamonds in the sun.

But still, we waited.

The ice would start to break away, making small holes through which we could finally see out.

But still, we waited.

And then, because it's a gut instinct to know the right time to flip on the windshield wipers, I'd look at my father and nod. He would nod back, and turn them on. If we were victorious, and we almost always were, the wipers would rid the entire windshield of ice in one quick motion. We would shout out with excitement, high five and make our way to school.

It wasn't until college that I learned ice scrapers existed.

Early in my relationship with my husband, we met at a coffee shop one Saturday morning. The romance was still new and giggly, and I was, perhaps, looking for the big red flag in an otherwise ideal mate. When we got up to the counter, I ordered my usual: a black coffee. The barista looked at me somewhat confused, but agreed to comply. Then Jim stepped up to the counter and ordered a venti, double-shot, peppermint mocha with extra whipped cream. The barista seemed relieved.

I panicked.

Despite his extremely fussy taste in coffee, we later married. And within our first year of marriage, we endured one of Oklahoma's harshest winters. I awoke one morning to unfamiliar sounds. Clawing and scraping sounds that only occur in terrifying campfire stories. I crept out of our bedroom, down the hall, into the living room and peeked out the window. There I saw a truly horrific sight: my husband, standing out in the snow, scraping ice from my windshield.

I flung open the door and yelled out to him: "Stop! STOP IT!" He looked up at me, confused as to why his extremely chivalrous act was eliciting such an angry reaction.

Later, seven years into marriage and with two daughters between us, we found ourselves talking one night about the struggle of parenting. Jim admitted that, at the end of a long day, he had such little energy that he dreaded putting the kids to bed. I confessed that I didn't mind putting the kids to bed, but that I dreaded getting up with them on Saturday mornings.

A deal was struck.

My husband has created his own routine with our daughters. Every Saturday morning he awakes when they do. He takes them down the stairs and makes a bowl of cereal for our oldest and a bottle for the baby. They sit together and color quietly or watch cartoons. But lately, when the weather is nice, he packs up both girls and walks to the neighborhood donut shop.

And even though my father no longer makes my breakfast, pours my coffee or drives me to school, my weekday mornings are still reserved for him. I make an intricate egg-based breakfast, like he did for me every morning growing up. I brew a large pot of coffee. I sit down at the table, and I talk to my dad. And while deep and meaningful conversation has now been replaced with witty text messages whizzing back and forth, the tradition remains.

And every Friday evening, as I put the girls to bed, I whisper in their ears that in the morning they will play together with their dad.

Oh how I envy them.

But I'm pleased by the thought that my husband is now providing our children with what my father has always given me:

A reason to get up in the morning.

The Grassy Knoll

For the past year, Jim and I struggled to grow a nice lawn around our new home. No matter what fertilizer, or watering routine, or rain dance we did, our grass refused to grow in anything but irregular and unimpressive patches. We spent so much time looking down at the grass, inspecting the soil, researching the seeds, and trying different aerators, we failed to ever look up.

But once we did, we realized the problem was not our seeds or our soil. The problem was our trees. Our small lot has four enormous trees, one of which is an historic sycamore with branches reaching out to shade the entirety of our backyard, and our neighbors' yards on either side. Our yard is so shady that the simple act of photosynthesis is impossible for our desperately darkened lawn.

It quickly became obvious that the only way we would ever grow the lush lawn of our dreams would be to trim back our trees. And we didn't just want some run-of-the-mill tree trimmer. We wanted a tree expert. The Lorax, if he made house calls. So I found a certified arborist to come assess the trees and advise us on how to get some sun on the desolate blades below.

He pulled into our driveway, stepped out of his car and gasped at the site of our trees. Two beautiful, enormous pin oaks in the front. And in the back, a wickedly twisted and deviant elm, and the massive sycamore. He went from tree to tree, placing his face close to the bark, squatting down around the roots, assessing the health of the leaves.

"Well," he finally said, "you have two options."

"Oh?" I asked.

"Yep. The trees or the lawn."

He went on to show me that on a lot our size, the trees and grass are competing for resources. He pointed to moss growing at the base of one of the oaks. This indicated that the trees were being overwatered in our attempt to hydrate the grass. And while trimming back the trees would allow more sunlight in, which could help the grass grow, we could never truly have a lush lawn unless we chopped the trees down completely.

"So," he said, "trees or lawn?"

Trees seemed like the obvious choice. The trees came first. They will far outlive us. The trees provide oxygen, shade, a habitat for squirrels and birds, and have—as it were—far deeper roots.

Lawns are, essentially, a waste of water. They are transient. Not truly a priority. And yet, grass provides curb appeal. A place to loll with my children on a warm day. A soft landing for birds. It provides proof we care about our property. And it keeps the soil in place. Soil, which nurtures the trees.

The arborist stood there awaiting my answer. He needed to know whether to take substantial branches from our beautiful canopies, or whether to trim them gently, tenderly and conservatively. He needed to know if I was a person who would team with the trees or go with the grass.

In the moment, I chose the trees.

As he looped a harness around his waist and powered the chainsaw, I got in my car to leave for work.

When I started my new position as a faculty member, my life dramatically changed in ways that might only appear subtle to others. On paper, perhaps, my life seems to be the same as it has been for years. I work for the same university. My commute is the same. I still have the same coworkers. I still park in the same spot and still pee in the same stall.

For seven years of my professional life I was a student, working in a dark basement office I shared with two other students. My mission in life was to take classes and research. My ultimate goal—graduation—was always so far away it was easier not to think long-range. So day in and day out I worked on small, achievable goals, like a term paper here, a research project there. Semester by semester, slowly chipping away at one large goal. My life at that time moved so slowly it sometimes felt as if it had stopped.

This isn't to say those seven years weren't fun and challenging. Or that the people with whom I shared a desk for that long aren't now among some of my closest friends. Because it was, and they are.

But until I stepped out and up into my new position, I had no idea how I had grown to feel about myself. Or my life. Because it's only in retrospect that I can see so clearly how isolating and lonely graduate school and researching were.

I enjoyed the courses and seeing classmates. I enjoyed conducting research out in the community. But I spent a majority of my days, my weeks, and the last seven years, in a basement office studying, analyzing data and writing. Or at home taking care of my young children, while I studied, analyzed and wrote during their naps. And while my children are certainly my life's work, they aren't the greatest conversationalists.

This shift in my life and in myself was so subtle I was unable to see the restrictions I felt. While I enjoyed my work, appreciated my growing knowledge, and valued my time with my small children, I found myself desperate for more human interaction. More conversation. More connection.

And so while my professional career was somewhat in a holding cell until graduation, I put my energy into developing an active and satisfying social life. One that would provide me with the interaction, conversation and connection I was lacking as a lowly graduate student in a basement office.

I planned parties, initiated happy hours, and scheduled lunches. I was able to respond immediately to text messages and emails. I could drop anything to be at the side of a friend or classmate or family member in need.

When my time as a student was over and my career began, I felt the sun finally shining on my face. I shifted overnight from an anonymous student worker in a basement to a visible faculty member with privileges.

Instantly my professional world became fertile ground for discussions, debates, meetings, presentations, recruiting and phone calls. I spend my days meeting with prospective students, advising current students, talking to administrators about program needs, answering calls about the program, responding to student emails, talking with faculty to set course schedules, presenting research, meeting with public affairs to promote our program, and talking with community leaders about partnerships.

And this is all before I get to class, where I stand in front of a room full of students and talking for three solid hours. For an extrovert, my job is a dream.

And yet I find myself, at the end of a long day, wishing I had time for happy hours. Realizing the days are too packed to schedule lunches. My energy is too zapped to plan a party. And my phone is full of unread messages.

While I'm finding myself immensely satisfied, my skills better used and my personality more fully leveraged than ever before, I miss the ways in which I once fed that need for interaction. Connection. Community.

My life as a student in the shady basement was a selfish and introspective time. I only had to worry about my research, my goals and myself. My life as a professor, warmed by the sun, is about many things bigger than me. No longer am I just thinking about my deadlines, my class work, my graduation date. Now I'm thinking about the students, the program, the university and the community. And once the sun shines on you, you have no choice but to spread and grow.

Yet I miss the chaotic time in my life when my girlfriends were my outlet. When my connection came from the woman down the street or the mothers' group I attended with my newborn. But now I find my energy so limited, my resources so strapped. I can't seem to nurture my professional aspirations and my sociability with equal measure.

When I returned home the day I met with the arborist, I found our trees delicately and beautifully trimmed. Their canopies were still full and lustrous, but they no longer drooped unnecessarily low to the ground, or hung heavily over the fence. Standing in the middle of my yard, I could see, for the first time, the sun dapple playfully across my shoes.

That evening, with a few limbs gone and our hope rising, my husband and I aerated the soil. We delicately and equally spread the seeds we'd spent time researching. We raked over the seedlings and watered the ground until the seeds had a cushiony bed of soft soil. Each morning that followed, I went outside and walked around the yard, inspecting the seeds as they nestled into the fertile soil. I monitored the sun at various points in the day to ensure it could poke through the thick branches above. We watered in careful intervals so as to give the yard enough, but not so much to drown the trees. We were mindful of the delicate balance.

And finally this morning, I saw—in the center of a patch of dirt we'd never been able to cultivate—a single blade of grass emerging triumphantly from beneath the soil.

I'm trying to temper my expectations. I remind myself that one sprig of grass in a barren spot doesn't mean a Masters quality golf course will follow. But at the very least, perhaps it is proof that the trees and the grass might both be able to pull from the same resources available to them within the confines of our small yard.

Somewhere down deep I truly believe that one day the grass will sprout and thicken and thrive. Perhaps it will be as lush and impressive as a forest.

And I hope I won't be able to see it for the trees.

Enough Already

My doctor came strolling into the hospital room—with me in bed feeding our newborn daughter—and shook my husband's hand in congratulations.

"So," he said as he took a seat in the room's rocking chair. "Let's talk birth control."

I let out a snort as my husband looked at him in disbelief.

"Oh," he said smiling as he swatted a hand. "I don't mean for use today, obviously."

"Well," I said, inhaling greatly as I looked at our baby, "this is our last one."

"Enough already, huh?" My doctor turned to my husband. "Okay, so are we making this permanent?"

"Yes," Jim replied. "Anyone you would recommend to do the procedure?"

The doctor took out a small note pad and quickly wrote down a few names and numbers. He told us most vasectomies book out about six months in advance, so it would be in our best interest to call as soon as possible. Not only that, but after the procedure was done, it would take a while for it to become effective.

"About 30 ejaculations before the vasectomy actually takes," the doctor said.

"Okay, so like a month," I stated.

He raised his eyebrows and looked at Jim.

"Oh!" My face began to feel hot. "I thought you meant days! Thirty days!" I stammered. "Trust me, that would *not* be a month."

The doctor let out a chuckle.

"I mean, it's not like it would be much longer than a month," I clarified. "Well, it just depends on our work schedules. And the kids. Or if it's sweeps week. You know how it goes when you're tired…"

"Meg, just stop," Jim interrupted, holding up his hand.

The doctor pulled out his pad again and wrote a prescription for birth control pills and handed it to me.

"Might also use condoms," he suggested. "You know," and here he clucked his tongue, "belt *and* suspenders."

A few days after returning home from the hospital with our beautiful new baby, Jim decided to call the urologist's office. Assuming it would take months to get an appointment, we were shocked to discover the urologist could see Jim the very next day.

I felt foolish and guilty accompanying my husband to a vasectomy consultation with a three-day-old baby. As if our next stop was the maternity ward to drop her off with a note pinned to her onesie: *Yeah, this just isn't for us. Thanks anyway!*

But when we got to the waiting room, I was surprised to see it was designed for children. Puzzles, toy cars and building blocks were in abundant supply. And children were *everywhere*. Climbing on furniture, ripping up magazines and pounding on the aquarium glass. If a man were wavering about whether or not to get a vasectomy, a urologist's waiting room would surely convince him.

I found it oddly enjoyable watching a room full of men, squeamish and red-faced, waiting for their names to be called by the nurse. After two pregnancies, during which Jim sat with me in the waiting rooms watching woman after woman waddle in to endure a cervical check, or a pap smear, or a transvaginal ultrasound, it was validating to see man after man hold his crotch protectively while trudging down the hall with the nurse.

My husband went back for the consultation by himself. I waited in the lobby, holding our darling infant child. Within minutes he was back. He reported that the doctor was no nonsense (fine with Jim) and not much of a talker (even better). He had given Jim a stack of pamphlets, a prescription for Valium and an appointment card for Thursday.

"*This* Thursday!?" I asked.

"Yeah," he shrugged. "He said most men want to do it around this time because there's a lot of sports on TV to watch during recovery."

"But you don't watch sports," I pointed out.

"Yeah, but there is a *Doctor Who* marathon this weekend."

"Thursday is too soon, Jim. I *just* had a baby!"

Jim consulted with the nurse to get the appointment pushed two months later. He came back and handed me the appointment card, and for the first time, looking down at the card with the date written in ink, I began to have doubts.

I never really had a vision in my head of what my family would look like. I never gave much thought to what kind of person my husband would be, though I had hoped for someone nice and smart. And I never gave much thought to how many children I would have, or what gender they would be. Just hoped for some who were nice and smart.

Jim, on the other hand, had all this in his head. Early in our courtship, while walking our dogs in the park, Jim—who is never shy about saying what he wants, especially on a third date—declared to me: "I would like to have two children. Girls, if possible."

In the moment I let out something that resembled nervous laughter, and slapped him on the arm playfully. But driving back to my apartment later that day, I realized it wasn't just a casual statement. Jim rarely makes any. It was a proposal. For a life he wanted to have with me.

And I realized I wanted it, too.

So it took me by surprise that after our second daughter was born—the daughter who perfectly completed the family we always wanted—I began to question our plans.

As if getting what you want makes you greedy.

The desire to have three children, it has occurred to me, is a societal pressure. I'm not suggesting that three isn't a great—perhaps even perfect—number of children. Many couples start their families with this number in mind. But I think many couples with two children are constantly asked when they will have the third. Yet those with three children are rarely asked about number four. For some reason, three is the number of children most people assume you and your partner will, maybe even should, have.

It's no wonder that three is the magic number in people's minds: it's the American sitcom formula. Take a couple, put them in a house with a staircase and give them three children. Perhaps it's better fodder for comedy because all personality stereotypes (see the Myers family) can be explored.

I'm not saying that television shapes how we lead our lives, but that goddamn Rachel haircut was everywhere. So there's something to be said about the way the mind receives messages on family (and hair) and how we, even unintentionally, demand our life imitate art.

And the fact that I'm the last of three children is not lost on me. My parents certainly could have stopped at two. They nearly did. Only after my brother was seven did they decide to strive for an American sitcom.

I, for one, applaud their choice.

But Jim and I had always agreed we wanted two children. And only two children. For a million reasons we had been over and over and over. And for us, in our lives and with our goals, it is the best decision. But I never imagined a decision that was already made would be so difficult to carry out.

So, in a gray, rainy fog, Jim and I slowly drove to the urologist's office. I knew deep down this was the right choice. A decision we made back when we were sane, rested, less emotional and not under the influence of a sweet, smiley newborn's alluring power. A decision we carefully considered from all angles. A decision made together.

And I was ready.

But as we drove through the rain, I wondered if Jim was having doubts. He sat so quietly beside me in the car that I wondered if, perhaps, he was finally allowing the emotion of the situation to take over all his logical plans.

We silently walked hand-in-hand into the building, checked in and took a seat in the waiting room.

"Meg..." Jim finally spoke.

"Yes?"

"I'm having some concerns."

"Oh Jim, it's okay! I'm struggling too. But I think what you said is right. We can do more for two than we can for three, and you are older than me and that's something to truly consider, and our career ambitions, and our desire to travel, and the fact that four fit easily in a booth and in a car, and we can afford to take them on a plane and they have each other and we aren't outnumbered and you've always wanted two girls and they are perfect—just the *best* kids—and this last pregnancy was so hard on my body, and all the stress of paying for childcare, and who would be able to watch *three* kids for any length of time when we've just had too much of them, and I don't even think I could come up with another baby name if I tried, and the house we just bought only has three bedrooms, even though I know we could technically convert the basement into a master but then we'd be two floors away from the kids and I'm just not sure that's the best idea—"

"No," he interrupted. "I'm having concerns that the Valium hasn't kicked in."

Before I could respond, the nurse called his name, he looked down sheepishly and slowly stood. As he went down the long narrow hallway, he glanced over his shoulder at me with a reassuring look that what he was about to do—and what it would mean—was the right decision.

Within twenty minutes, he came shuffling back into the waiting room, his tall, slender body slightly hunched over.

"Well?" I asked.

"You'll be pleased to know," he said, offering a weak smile, "I had my feet in stirrups the whole time."

I suppose there was never really all that much doubt in my mind about stopping at two children. I guess it's more about the difficulty of ending this phase of our life. I'll never experience another pregnancy. I'll never decorate another nursery. I'll never give birth again. And while it is difficult to let go of those aspects of our life, I'm more excited by what's to come.

Just still a little surprised how quickly we went from that day in the park with our dogs, to now.

And that's the thing about it. The hardest part wasn't saying "enough already."

The hardest part is we have reached enough.

Already.

May/December

Light opens on a dimly lit restaurant. A couple sits at a small table for two, center stage. They are surrounded by several other tables with people sitting at them and eating. There is a subtle sound of conversation and silverware clanking. A waiter, an older gentleman, approaches the couple.

Waiter: So good to see you again.

Wife: Yes. [*smiles*] Like clockwork.

Waiter: Would you care for your usual drinks?

Husband: Yes, please. Extra dirty. And *four* olives.

Waiter: Certainly. M'am? The Zinfandel?

Wife: You know it.

Waiter: Excellent. I'll put your drink orders in and bring you some fresh bread.

Husband: Thank you.

Waiter leaves table and exits stage left.

Husband: [*sighs and smiles*] This was a long week.

Wife: You say that every week.

Husband: I know, I know. I don't mean to be so cranky.

Wife: You're the perfect kind of cranky. Someone who isn't really cranky, but thinks he is.

Husband stretches legs out to side of table. Sits back.

Husband: You were quiet on the drive. What's the story there?

Wife: Oh, I dunno...Lot on my mind.

Husband: Well, start somewhere.

Wife: Johnny Depp fatigue?

Husband: Start somewhere else.

Wife: [*pauses, fiddles with napkin*] Do you remember the other day we both had off and I wanted to get a manicure?

Husband: Of course. I dropped you off at that place around the corner.

Wife: Right. You talked with me for a bit and then left to get a coffee.

Husband: Yeah…?

Wife: Well, when you left, the manicurist said [*mimics Vietnamese accent*] "Ahh, he much, much older than you."

Husband: [*snorts*] Oh? Much? That's funny.

Wife: I know. I told her "much" was a bit strong, but yeah.

Husband: Normally that doesn't bother you…

Wife: Oh, *that* didn't bother me. It's what she said next. [*mimics again*] "When he came in here I couldn't believe what a *man* he was."

> Husband laughs out loud with a big, one syllable hoot.

Wife: Seriously.

Husband: You don't get manlier than me.

Wife: She said you were *elegant*. Masculine and elegant. Like you're some kind of wild, beautiful stallion running through midtown.

Husband: Fairly accurate description.

Wife: She was thinking, "How did this girl with the yoga pants and rough cuticles land *that*?"

Husband: She wasn't thinking that. You're gorgeous. And besides, who cares?

Wife: I know, I know...But the one day I don't shower...

Husband: To be fair, I shouldn't have worn my tweed blazer. Too dangerous.

> *Waiter delivers the two drinks and a basket of bread.*
> *Husband takes a sip of his martini.*

Wife: My body after kids. [*snorts*] I now sneeze-pee and your waist has gotten *smaller*.

Husband: You're more beautiful now than when we got married. Besides, you're the first to say that looks don't matter. You stress it to the girls all the time.

Wife: Oh, that's just what people say, like "I gave at the office," or "I love working out."

Husband: Wait, you don't like working out? It's like I don't even know you.

Wife: Not caring about looks is what people do when they aren't known for their beauty.

Husband: Stop it.

Wife: No.

Husband: No, I mean stop drinking my martini. You've got your own drink.

Waiter comes back to the table, takes orders. The orders are not heard, just the sound of muted muttering over background music. Waiter leaves, music fades.

Wife: So, while she's finishing my nails, she says, [*mimics again*] "Aww, you very very lucky lady."

Husband: This sounds mildly racist…

Wife: I mean, I know I'm lucky…

Husband: [*smiling*] You are.

Wife: Stop. I know. I know you are great. But *she* doesn't know that. Doesn't know your personality or what you are like as a husband and father. You didn't even do anything and I'm "lucky."

Husband: I find it odd you are telling me this story so much after the fact. That was over a week ago. You usually tell me your thoughts the moment you have them. Even if I'm in the bathroom.

Wife: I know. It just built over time, I guess. Lately I've had a lot of people stressing to me how lucky I am to have you. Like I'm somehow unaware…or unworthy. [*pauses, looks around*] Or just on the verge of ruining it.

Husband: I'm the lucky one here.

Wife: Oh…not really…The other day the diaper genie was full. And I stood there looking at it forever, thinking: I have no clue how to empty the damn thing. [*sips wine*] Three and a half years, two kids, a million diapers later and I've never once changed the bag.

Husband: [*shrugs*] Least I can do.

Wife: Stop it. This is why people think *I'm* the lucky one.

Husband: You aren't. I am.

Wife: Obviously. [*takes sip*] Still, everyone acts like you just dropped from the damn sky. But I'm the one who recognized how amazing you are…and I pursued the relationship when others might not have.

Husband: [*smiling*] Might not have?

Wife: You know…[*waving a hand between them*]…the age difference. Plus, you remember your hair back then, right?

Husband: Point taken.

Wife: People act like I should count my lucky stars.

Husband: Who? Who acts like that?

Wife: [*pauses*] My mother.

> *Waiter refills water glasses. Husband smiles, reaches across table to grab the wife's hand.*

Wife: I like that shirt. You're cute and I love you.

Husband: I love you more. And I'm always happy to be out with you on my arm.

Wife: Our relationship only works if people see me as the young trophy wife that I am.

Husband: They do. I was as disappointed as anyone when I figured out you had brains.

Wife: I married older thinking it would come with wealth.

Husband: Tough break. [*eats a bite of bread*] You ready for class tomorrow night?

Wife: Oh…I guess.

Husband: Where's your normal enthusiasm? You typically can't sleep the night before class because of excitement.

Wife: No, no. I'm excited…

Husband: But?

Wife: Oh...it's just...Well, the other day one of my students said I was really *entertaining*.

Husband: That's awesome.

Wife: Yeah. If I were an *entertainer*. I just wonder if they are learning.

Husband: Oh please. The first rule of teaching is: engage the students.

Wife: The second rule is: don't sleep with your students.

Husband: Actually, let's go ahead and call *that* the first rule. Maybe the only rule.

Wife: Got it.

Husband: You've had lots of experience in the classroom...But this is your first semester carrying the weight of it all. The administrative part, the research part, the advising part. Give yourself time to adjust. Grow into the role.

Wife: You're doing everything you can not to point out how early I am in my career—how green and young I am—aren't you?

Husband: Did the waiter card you? [*looking around the restaurant*] He should have...

> *Wife takes another long, pointed drink of his martini.*

Husband: A real woman can look past her hatred of olives to make a point.

Wife: [*pauses, sighs*] I can't even process it all right now. I mean, I've never been more satisfied and excited...the kids, the job...you...But now I feel like I'm...I dunno...failing in other areas.

Husband: Such as?

Wife: My friends for one. Just don't have as much time, or energy, for everything I used to do with them…

Husband: Like what?

Wife: When's the last time I hosted a Girls' Night? I'm busting my ass trying to make it all work. Trying to fit it all in. It's like Whack-A-Mole.

Husband: Cut yourself some slack. Or no one else will.

Wife: I can't. And they don't.

Husband: Well *I* do. I actually like when you're distracted. I get more reading done.

Wife: [*laughs, takes a drink*] You are good for me.

Husband: You're even better for me. Just look at my hair.

Wife: I'm going to check in on the girls. [*rummages around in purse for her phone*]

Husband: They're fine.

Wife: I know. [*still rummaging*] But Lunny was a little fussy earlier. I just want that tooth to pop through already.

Husband: You're so bonded to her.

Wife: [*looks up from phone, furrows brow*] I'm bonded to both of them.

Husband: No, I know. It's just been so different this time around. [*pauses*] You're incredible with them. You know that, right?

Wife: Oh I guess. [*continues texting, then looks up*] Sometimes it's like, I can't even breathe when I look at them, I'm so in love. And they are both so sweet and so cute. But then…[*pauses*]. When they are *both* crying…at the same time…both needing me in the *same* moment…I just want to walk out the front door, get in the car and leave.

Husband: Can I come?

Wife: Better not. I'm a lone wolf.

Husband: Well, by the time you found your car keys in that purse, they would have probably stopped crying.

Wife: [*holds up her purse*] This mess is my maternal instinct.

> *They are silent for a moment. Both take a few sips of their drinks.*

Wife: Lunny makes me feel like a good mom.

Husband: You are.

Wife: No, I mean, I know I am by common, rational standards. But she just makes me *believe* I'm good. Like I have instincts. She's just so easily comforted by me.

Husband: We all are.

Wife: Yeah, right. I've never felt it was a strength I have as a mother. At least not with Cakes. [*looks at him for a beat*] I wish I could be more like you are with her. More patient.

Husband: I'm only good with her because she's a little version of you. Louder, but basically the same.

Wife: That's part of my struggle…I can barely deal with myself half the time. I've just convinced myself we will always fight.

Husband: Yeah, but it's good to fight. Especially the way you two do it. I mean, come on, even the little fight you have about who loves each other more is adorable.

Wife: [*laughs*] I love to see her lose it when she says "I love you most" and I just throw my hands up and say "You win!"

Husband: She's lucky to be like you. And that's why she and I get along well. I'm as intrigued by her as I am by you.

Wife: I think you mean *entertained.*

Husband laughs.

Wife: [*looks down at phone again*] Okay, she wrote back. Baby girl is out. Cakes is painting. [*sighs, relieved, then pauses and drinks*] Are you ready for the executive retreat next week?

Husband: Oh, I guess…[*looks off*] It's sometimes a little bit of a challenge.

Wife: Your job? Or being married to me?

Husband: Both. But also, just knowing I'm the same age as the others…

Wife: What does that mean?

Husband: Just being a man in my age group…

Wife: As opposed to a woman? Or a man in *my* age group?

Husband: [*shrugs*] Maybe it's more about having young kids…

Wife: Oh! [*she claps once*] The *Vanity Fair* came yesterday and Angelina Jolie is on the cover.

Husband: Yes, isn't there a Philip Roth interview in there?

Wife: Yes, yes. [*she swats a hand*] I put it on your nightstand. But did you see the cover? The headline says something like, "An In-depth Interview with *Mrs. Pitt.*"

Husband: [*laughs*] Burn.

Wife: I know, right? [*takes a sip*] I mean, the world has referred to Gavin Rossdale as the "Bush front man" for 20 years. Bush hasn't released an album since the early 90s. They aren't even a band anymore.

Husband: No...they got back together a few years ago. I think they have a new album out...

Wife: Oh...Well. They called him the "Bush front man" for so damn long the band *had* to get back together. They are lucky to have that expectation on them.

Husband: Wonder what Mrs. Rossdale thinks about that.

Wife: [*laughs, eats a bite of bread*] So anyway, the retreat. What were you saying?

Husband: Oh...I'm the same age as all of them but they all have grown kids. So flying off to a retreat in the woods is no big deal for them or the wives they leave behind. Their kids can drive themselves to school. The wives aren't stuck changing diapers.

Wife: Don't worry, women can feel resentment at any stage of life. I'm sure those wives have plenty to go on.

Husband: I can only imagine...

Wife: Besides, those guys are probably wishing they had waited longer to have children, like you did. You had the advantage of building your career *before* your children came along. [*pauses, looks off*] You don't have to struggle with being early in your career *and* early in parenthood. [*takes a sip*] Besides, our two babies keep you young.

Husband: Then how do you explain how much grayer I've gotten since Cakes was born?

Wife: Elegance.

> *Waiter brings a tray full of plates to the table.*
> *Places plates in front of the couple.*

Husband: We need to baby proof a bit more. Lunny is on the move now.

Wife sighs heavily. Cuts into her steak. Takes a bite. Sits back.

Husband: What? Am I doing it again? Being overly cautious?

Wife: Always. But it's not that. It's just the monotony of it all.

Husband: Of life?

Wife: Yeah, well, life and parenting. It's like, I do the dishes *every* day. Sometimes twice a day. And I'm washing those damn bottles and thinking: This will only last until tomorrow. Then I have to do it all over again. And the laundry. It's never ending. So many tiny pairs of *Frozen* underwear to wash and dry and put away. It's adorable and maddening all at once. [*pauses*] I know I need to savor the moments...but I just get tired of the monotony.

Husband: And yet, we lose our minds when something goes awry. Breaks our routine. Like a cold. Or teething.

Wife: I know...But even the chaos feels monotonous.

Lights go down for a moment and then back up again. Time has passed. The waiter comes and clears plates. Sets down a cup of coffee in front of the husband and places the bill in the middle of the table.

Husband: [*takes a cautious sip of his coffee and sits back*] We don't read enough plays.

Wife: [*rolls eyes*] Oh god...

Husband: We used to read a lot of plays. And go see a lot of plays.

Wife: Yes, and get ten hours of sleep a night...and go to the movies...and drink at bars....

Husband: I know, I know. I just really think we need to read more plays.

Wife: Why? Oh, because we just saw *Birdman?*

Husband: No. I mean, that reminded me, but I just really like reading plays.

Wife: I guess. They are just always so depressing. Who cares about the drunken malaise of the upper-middle class?

Husband: Okay then, Shakespeare?

Wife: Me thinks no.

Husband: We can read something more contemporary. Maybe find a play with just a couple of characters and read it to each other.

Wife: Naked?

Husband: Whatever works.

> *They sit back and look around the restaurant.*

Wife: [*breaking the silence*] You always do that, you know? You always seem so nostalgic for the past. For the things we used to do. Always wanting to recapture the past.

Husband: Maybe. [*pauses*] But you're always wanting to move forward at lightning speed. Tackling project after project like you are blissfully unaware of how long life is.

> *The couple is silent again. Husband pays the bill.*
> *The waiter comes up quietly to retrieve the tray of cash.*

Husband: [*to waiter*] I don't need any change.

Waiter: Thank you both. We will see you next week, yes?

Wife: [*smiling*] You know it.

> *Stage darkens. A light appears stage right on a rounded,*
> *blue exterior door. The couple exits through the door.*

Wife: [*rubs hands together rapidly*] Burrrr!

Husband: I know, it's brutal. [*helps wife into her coat, holds her in an embrace, rests his chin on top of her head*]

Wife: Everyone is right. I am the lucky one. [*looks up at him*] I just hate that they all know it.

Husband: They know nothing.

Wife: All good things in my life stem from you, you know.

Husband: Hush. You're gushing.

Wife: [*looks up at the sky*] I didn't realize it was going to be this cold tonight.

Husband: I hate winter.

Wife: So cranky...

Husband: I'm more lovable in the summer.

Wife: Says who?

Husband: Your manicurist.

Lights fade as the couple walks slowly, hand-in-hand, off stage right.

END SCENE

Lather, Rinse, Repeat

T his is the cycle:

I'll grow my hair out very long. Not quite as long as it was in high school, which was *Splash* like, but long by modern standards. I marvel at the length. I love pulling it up at night to wash my face. Love how it looks spiral-curled—like a woman on a procedural show. And I love how it feels when it falls on my shoulders or when my husband runs his hands through it. Love it fully, for about three months.

Then one day, after I finish blow-drying it for 20 minutes, and am dripping with sweat, I storm out of the bathroom and yell, "That's it! I can't take it any more! I'm chopping it off!" It has been my experience that women don't get "hair cuts." They "chop it off."

So I get an emergency session with my stylist and she chops off my hair into a bob. And when I see the bob I gasp with excitement and exclaim, "I love it! *This* is how my hair should *always* look."

I love the volume of the bob. How quickly it dries. The compliments I get. But then, one day, after spending 20 minutes with the flat iron trying to fight with my cowlick and get the back to "bob" just so, I storm out of the bathroom and yell, "That's it! I can't take it any more! I'm growing it out!"

And so it goes.

My stylist avoids being openly annoyed as I plop down, exasperated, in her chair, demanding she chop it off after she spent a year holding my hand through a rough grow out. And she hides her skepticism when I bounce in excitedly showing her a picture of Keri Russell (early season one) and demand that she "make me look like her!"

As a child, until the age of two, I was bald. When the hair finally started to grow in, it was cotton white. Any objective passerby would agree it was adorable. Especially when my mother pulled it into ever-so-slightly curling pigtails. My hair was a defining characteristic.

My best friend, whom I met the first day of preschool, was a redhead. I loved her immediately. Together, we were the towhead and carrot top who wore macaroni necklaces and played at length with *My Little Pony* toys.

We were special. Our hair conveyed this.

After the car accident, my hair was such a tangled mess of blood and rocks and sticks and glass that the doctors insisted on shaving it off completely. My mother refused. When they fought her, saying it was so matted and tangled that it would never unfurl, she said she wanted the chance to try. And so, for the four weeks I was bound to the hospital bed, 800 miles from home, my mother worked meticulously to unravel my blonde mane.

This was our daily activity.

She would pick gingerly at the ends, finding that if she could just get a one-inch-by-one-inch section of hair untangled, we would ultimately be successful.

She sprayed it and combed it until my head ached so tremendously she would have to stop for the day. And eventually, near the time I was to be discharged, she had picked out every piece of gravel and every shard of glass and successfully brushed out the entire three feet of my white, silky hair.

Then she called for shampoo.

And it was a celebration. Nurses piled into the room to watch as the stylist rinsed the dried blood and then combed my hair out in a fan shape on my pillow to allow everyone to take pictures. It was the biggest of victories.

My mother had saved my hair.

And for the rest of my childhood, we had such fun with it. Crimping it for school pictures (yes, I was super cool), braiding it for gymnastic tournaments, having it professionally styled for my brother's wedding. Buying all kinds of scrunchies and banana clips and mastering the side ponytail.

But as I got older, my hair progressively got darker. It broke my mother's heart. I missed it, sure, but I knew that it was challenging for my mother to see the youth disappear from my hair.

So, after high school graduation, I began highlighting.

It started simply enough. A few foils every semester break from college. I was *maintaining* the color of my youth. It just took a few streaks of bleach every six months to keep the magic alive. But as every woman knows, a few innocent highlights are a gateway dye.

When I graduated college, and took a job in a new city, I was pining for a fresh start with my hair to match the fresh start in my life. I sat down in the hydraulic chair, wrapped in a cape, and said, "Chestnut me."

In I went as a (bubbly?) blonde, out I came as a (sultry?) brunette. The ladies in the shop loved it. They oohed and aahed, and I walked out of there with such confidence that when I got back to my apartment, the guy from 12G flirted with me in the elevator. And I flirted back.

But I woke up the next morning with a massive hair hangover. I called my sister before sunrise, telling her I couldn't go to work. I was too embarrassed. People would hate it. And also, what colors of clothes go with my hair now? White? Pink seems to clash. Can I still pull off black? How the hell should I do my makeup?

At work, most everyone was shocked by my new look. Though they had only known me three months, they seemed betrayed. Disgusted, maybe. And in walked my boss, a powerful, scary woman—a Joan Rivers kind of feminist—who contended that part of a woman's role is to look as beautiful as she can. She herself was a blonde, and maintained her highlights every two weeks for an astronomical cost. She came up to me, touched my hair, sighed heavily, and said for all to hear: "Why the hell would you do this to yourself?"

164

But that was nothing compared to my mother's reaction. She had no words. She looked around at me, trying to find a place for her eyes to land. She mumbled something about my shoes and then excused herself to cry in the hall closet. It would have been better for me to confess I was knocked up by some drummer out on parole.

It's been 10 years and she *still* brings it up.

So after the Chestnut Incident of 2005, I began to allow my stylist to do more creative tricks with color in order to find a balance between the color my mother knew from my childhood and the color my hair had turned in adulthood.

But after years of trying different coloring, all to hearken back to what it once was, I've become resentful of my own head. Tired of all the effort. The cost. The need to please my mother.

When my older daughter was born, she had faint wisps of hair. And for two and a half years, not much more. But slowly, one lock of hair grew out on the side of her head, just above her right ear. It was nearly translucent.

And it curled.

By the time my daughter turned three she had a full head of bright white ringlets.

She is known for many things. Her large, blue eyes. Her long, dark lashes. Her effervescence. Her sense of humor. Her grasp of language. Her imagination. Her empathy.

But most of all, my older daughter is known for her crazy, curly, white hair.

I catch myself twisting her hair around my fingers as we watch a movie together. And in the mornings, when I comb out the tangles, I always take a second to bury my nose in her curls.

My younger daughter was born with slightly more hair. And though it's still very short and scarce, it's very clearly strawberry blonde. Her lashes are a deep auburn.

Or maybe it's wishful thinking.

For another pair of special girls, one as white-headed as I once was, the other as gingered as my best friend.

And I try each day not to obsess too much about their hair. Not to fall too in love with my eldest's curls or my youngest's color. I force myself to imagine them in 20 years with different styles. Different colors. And constantly remind myself that the majestic look of their hair right now is simply the look of their childhood.

But not necessarily a guarantee for their entire lives.

I often wonder how differently things would have gone if my mother had just let the doctors shave me bald. Perhaps my hair would have grown in just as blonde and silky as before. Or maybe it would have grown in thicker, darker, maybe even curly.

I'm not sure how my hair would have grown back in, but I do know it would have felt more like mine than the head of hair I have now. And I wouldn't still feel the need to have my hair be a constant gift to my mother.

But I respect and admire her decision in the hospital to try to keep what I had. Preserve what was precious. Protect what was perfect. And however burdensome, my hair will always be an extremely intense experience that she and I shared more than two decades ago.

And a really good lesson in motherhood: every inch of my children is worth fighting for.

Home School

D espite what many people think, I did *not* marry Chad Morgan. I don't mind the assumption; I just want to set the record straight. Because, since leaving my sleepy little hometown in rural Oklahoma more than 15 years ago, this is still an assumption people make when they hear me use my new last name.

Chad came from a family of athletes. He is the middle child of three smart, handsome, and talented boys, all well over six feet tall. John Carl is the eldest, Brett is the youngest. I met Chad in the first grade. He and I were the best students in Mrs. Williams' class.

Sensing we were bored with the curriculum, she challenged us to a read-off. Whoever read the most books over the course of the year won a pizza party. Which, ironically, was to be shared with the rest of the class.

So for the entire first grade, Chad and I went to our corners, furiously trying to read the most books. Sadly, he defeated me in what I think everyone agreed was a Cinderella story. I still vividly remember that I read 148 books to Chad's 152.

Later, in high school, Chad and I were both in advanced placement English and calculus. English was my strongest subject (despite, or maybe because of, losing to him in the first grade); his was math. Over the summer we were assigned *The Old Man and the Sea*. While I read a dozen books that summer, Hemingway wasn't one of them. Chad *did* read it. Maybe even twice. But on the essay test he got an 87% while I scored almost perfect having just read the book jacket.

In calculus, however, Chad didn't even have to try. Everyone in the class made A's, including two classmates whom I tutored, and I could still only eek out a low B. This greatly upset my father. Did he want me to be a mathematician? Did it embarrass him that I had the worst grade in the class? Even if that grade was a "B"?

One evening, after a particularly horrendous test, I proudly told my parents over dinner that I had made an 84%. My dad kept chewing his meat until it was finished, put down his fork, wiped his mouth and asked, "What did Chad make?"

I still have no idea if my dad was kidding in that moment. But joke or not, it's still an issue between us. When I graduated magna cum laude from college, my dad leaned over and said, "Chad graduated *summa*." When I got accepted into my doctoral program, my dad responded to the news with "Isn't Chad in optometry school? They make better money than professors." And in the hospital after the birth of my child, my father held my newborn daughter in his hands, tears streaming down his face and blubbered, "I bet Chad could do this."

When you grow up in such a small town, which appears to offer so little in the way of diversity, opportunity and experience, you can't help but be excited at the prospect of getting the hell outta there.

To dream of challenges greater than Chad.

I enjoyed growing up where I did. Was proud of my upbringing. Loved my childhood home and all the country air. I liked my neighbors and my classmates, my fellow Girl Scouts, and the friends whose birthday parties I attended for 17 years. I liked high school enough, and I thought we received a good education. But I always felt there was so much more outside the tiny town.

I think maybe we all felt this way.

In a town like this, friendships are formed in toddlerhood and carried through until adulthood. I've reconnected with many of my former classmates over parenthood. With several others, I never lost touch. But growing up, it was a mission of mine to move away to a college where no one I knew was going. It was crucial that I study abroad in a land far, far away. It was imperative that I start a career in a bigger city with lots of art and jobs and high-rise apartment buildings. And it was not a question that I would marry someone who had never once been to my hometown.

During my time abroad I spent a weekend in Wales with my European friends. After horseback riding all day on a foggy beach, we settled into the town bar for drinks. When the bartender asked where I was from, I rolled my eyes and said, "The States." More sheepishly I added, "Oklahoma." With my voice even lower, "A very tiny rural town with only two stoplights." To which she replied, "My heavens, that sounds magical!"

When I found a man to marry, a different Morgan, a man who himself was well traveled and educated and cultured, I was warmed by how truly important it was for him to meet my parents, to see where I grew up, to understand my childhood and to fall completely in love with it.

A town in which the parents have bonds that reach far beyond their children's participation in football. A town where the movie theater only has three screens. A town with lots of mom and pop shops standing strong against Wal-Mart. A town where the sight of a person riding horseback down Main Street isn't unusual. A town in which you describe people not by the content of their character, but by their relationship to the postman. A town in which my father co-founded the Calf Fry Festival, the long-running, heavily-attended, event of the year in which local businesses vie for the best tasting fry-battered testicles. I can't make this shit up.

But the quaint, pastoral town, like any other town, isn't safe from poverty, or domestic violence, or racism, or ignorance or hatred or crime. So, thankfully, it only offered one option for school. Every kid—rich, poor, black, white, daughter-of-the-postman, never-heard-of-the-postman—were all collected in one building. And no amount of dual immersion, European-based, top-rated, nationally-certified, award-winning pedagogy can top what that organic diversity provides its students.

In my class of nearly 100 people, there is ample evidence of success. A couple of doctors, a few lawyers, a college professor, a handful of teachers and nurses and dental hygienists, an abundance of people with advanced degrees, and lots and lots of people who stayed in the town and have started and maintained successful businesses. And most people have husbands or wives or loving partners, and lots have children of their own, some of whom are beginning to make their way through the same school district we all left more than a decade ago.

So now, when I see an old friend from high school or someone from my hometown, it shouldn't surprise me that their first question is: Did you marry Chad? Or, no, Brett? Oh wait, it was probably John Carl, right?

It's not that people from my hometown truly believe that there is only one Morgan family in the world, or that they think Chad or Brett or John Carl was particularly well suited for me. It's more that they think of our town first, maybe only, and can't imagine why we would need to search for anything beyond it.

I always liked that everyone knew who I was because of my last name. They know my father, or my mother, or went to school with my siblings, or maybe they even know of me personally. My last name was my connection to my home, my badge of honor, my stake in the land, proof that I existed once in a community that was as loving and inescapable as mine. I was worried I'd lose that a little when I took my husband's name. But, because of the identical nomenclature, Morgan ties me back to Chad, which, in essence, ties me back home.

I know I should want more for my daughters than I had for myself. For her to have a better childhood, a stronger education, more interesting friends, greater opportunities. But looking back at what I had, that just seems impossible.

Unless one day Chad has a child, with whom one of my daughters falls madly in love and marries.

Or at least slaughters at the Science Fair.

Thanksgiving:
A Series of Unfortunate Events

It is Thanksgiving. Roughly 6 a.m. I awake to a shooting pain on the top of my hand. A pain that is precise, small, deep and commanding. I am on my side, one arm under my pillow and the other up under my chin. My eyes flutter open to see, mere inches from my face, a black creature of some kind on my hand. Not knowing what it is, and too groggy to process the information my eyes are absorbing, I instinctually—and with the adrenaline of a mother lifting a car off her child—raise my other hand up from under the pillow and swat the creature away with rapid and blunt force.

My eyes close again. The pain is getting worse. Tighter, smaller, but stronger. A specific point on the top of my hand where the crease makes my wrist. I try to ignore the pain and allow sleep to take back over. My mind begins to wander. What was that large, black creature I saw so briefly before heroically batting it across the room? It seemed black as night. And...triangular? Fan shaped? What if—I begin to panic and my eyes shoot open—it was a spider?

Thinking of my two precious children sleeping down the hall, and fearing the spider—who has now been batted toward the door and could be making his way to their sweet fleshy skin—I sit up. I look at the floor beside the bed. I know I swatted in this direction; where is it?

"Meg..." Jim grumbles through a deep slumber. "What are you doing?"

"Something bit me," I whisper, poised and ready to pounce.

"What do you mean...something..." He dozes momentarily before awakening to finish, "Bit you?"

With my eyes still combing the floor of our bedroom, I hold up my arm so he can see my wrist.

"It doesn't look like you've been bitten," he exclaims. "It looks like you've been shot!"

Only then do I think to finally look at my wrist. I bring it close to my face and see the damage. A large lump, swelling by the second, and in the center: the bullet hole.

"Mother of god!" I declare, and pull my legs up under me as though the bed is my life raft in a sea of sharks.

Jim springs up and quickly makes his way around to my side of the bed, quietly and intently searching for the lone gunman.

"Well, how are we supposed to find anything over here?!" he huffs. His eyes dart around the various piles of magazines, shoes, maternity clothes intended for donation, used contact lenses, and an open piece of luggage I've yet to fully unpack.

"Are you freaking kidding me? Now's not the time!" I yell. "Find that creature!"

Jim rifles through the mess, tossing aside socks and scarves and magazines like a mower churning through a pile of leaves.

"Found it!" he cries.

And there, against the baseboard, having clearly been knocked across the room and slammed against the wall with the force of a maniac, twitching in a state of shock, is the biggest ass wasp I've ever seen.

Afternoon

The pain on my wrist is subsiding slightly. The swelling is waning. The bullet hole is closing. I'm rushing around to prepare the house and my little family for a Thanksgiving visit from my in-laws.

I sit for a moment with a pad of paper to go over my list of things to do today: I've put the finishing touches on lunch. I've cleaned the house from top to bottom. I've bathed both the girls. I've done two loads of laundry and a load of dishes. I've adorned the house with all my favorite holiday decor. I've lit candles. I've set the table.

And, I've victoriously watched a four pound wasp spin around and around in circles as it made its way down our toilet.

I've nothing left to do but shower.

The girls are resting quietly. I contemplate a glass of wine, but think better of it. I make my way upstairs. I take a long, steamy shower, mentally enumerating what is left to do before my husband's parents ring the doorbell.

I realize I'm ready.

I get out of the shower and walk into our bedroom, still worried I'll find a hive, but instead, find my husband snoring on our bed. Poor thing, I think. He helped capture my predator in the early morning hours. He helped pull the holiday decorations from the attic. He helped bathe the girls. And he was the executioner who pulled the handle on the toilet after I happily tossed in the big, black creature by one of its twitchy wings.

I decide to let him sleep.

I dress quickly, towel dry my hair, and back out of our room. I carefully close the door and creep toward my oldest daughter's room. She's sleeping peacefully. Heavily. Beautifully. I stand in her doorway feeling tight in my chest.

Today is Thanksgiving. It's about being thankful. It's about family. I watch her chest rise and fall with shallow breath. I need to dry my hair. I need to put on makeup. But I can't seem to leave her doorway.

Impulsively, filled with the spirit of Thanksgiving, I decide I want to lie down with her and rest a bit. I tip toe over to her bed. She doesn't move an inch. I carefully shimmy my way onto the mattress beside her. She doesn't move an inch. I carefully thread my arm behind her head and bring her close to my chest. She doesn't move an inch. We lie there, embracing, peaceful, calm. My eyes begin to feel heavy. And just as I drift off to sleep, thankful for this moment, reveling in my existence, my child's eyes pop open and she realizes I'm beside her.

"MOMMY!" she declares with the excitement of a thousand three-year-olds.

And as she lifts her body to hug me back, so happy I'm beside her, she rams her big, hard head smack into my mouth.

I cry out in pain. My lip immediately begins to throb and swell. I break our embrace and run out of her room and down the stairs and into the kitchen to grab ice. I quickly wrap a cube in a paper towel. I hear my daughter crying from her bed, heartbroken she has hurt me and that our snuggle time is over.

I get the bleeding to stop. With ice melting in my hand, I make my way to the stairs, thinking I have time to get to my child before her sobs wake her father and sister from their slumber. As my foot hits the first step, the door bell rings.

I open the door to see my in-laws standing bright-eyed and 10 minutes early.

"Oh dear!" my mother-in-law exclaims. "What happened to your face?!"

Evening

My in-laws have left. The welt on my wrist is nearly gone. My swollen lip has subsided enough that I no longer lisp.

The baby sleeps peacefully upstairs. Holiday music plays softly in the living room as my oldest child paints quietly beside the fireplace. My husband pours me a well-deserved glass of wine.

Despite the feast at lunch, my child complains of hunger.

"I'll make you macaroni," I say as I gently rub her head.

"Oh! I *love* macaroni," she says, eyes as big as saucers.

This I know. Of all things I make her, she loves my macaroni and cheese the most. It secretly thrills me to make it for her, even though I truly hate to cook.

I turn on the stove and place a pot of water on it. Jim brings me my glass and we stand in the kitchen talking about the day.

His parents were good. The visit was nice. The girls were the model grandkids. We feel thankful.

My daughter wanders into the kitchen and hugs my leg as I pour the noodles into the boiling water. I bend down to kiss her. The day is winding down.

I pull a noodle from the rolling water, blow on it and bring it to my mouth. The pasta is ready.

"Go get in your seat, sweetie," I say to her, and she makes her way into the dining room and crawls up into her chair.

I turn off the range. The flame extinguishes. I find the lid to the pot and place it on top. I bring the pot to the sink and prepare to drain the water. But as I tip the pot up on its side, my stung wrist begins to throb and my hand slips slightly. Instantly, boiling water is rushing over my other hand and I yelp, jumping back in pain. As I do this, my finger touches the boiling hot pot and is instantly seared.

I throw the lid, and the pot, and what's left inside of it, angrily into the sink. I storm out of the kitchen holding my finger.

"Run it under cold water!" Jim yells from the kitchen as he gathers wet, hot noodles from the sink. Minutes later, my finger—still beet red—feels better. Good enough to carry out the rest of my child's favorite meal. I stir in the cheese sauce. I scoop out a portion for my daughter and put it in front of her at the table.

There I sit, wasp stung wrist, fat lip and burned finger, watching my child inhale the pasta I made for her.

"How's your wrist?" Jim asks across the table.

"Better," I say somberly.

"And your finger?" he asks, looking at the ice pack I have resting on it.

"Better," I shrug.

"And your lip?" my sweet child asks between bites.

"Better," I respond.

"Good," she says with her mouth full. "I'm sorry I did that."

I laugh. Impressed by her in a whole new way.

"And mommy..." she says quietly.

"Yes," I say, bringing the wine to my lips.

"Thank you for this," she says, pointing to her plate.

And for a moment, I think her sweetness, her innocence, her beauty and her kindness are enough to erase all the pain I have endured today.

And they just almost are.

For that, I am thankful.

Thorn in Her Paw

Our three-year-old came home from school one day with a splinter in her thumb. In her mind, this was the most fascinating event that had ever happened in her life.

She explained, in great detail, how she got the splinter on a piece of bamboo during craft time. She talked endlessly about how her friends had gathered around to share in her excitement and gawk at her finger. She gabbed on and on about her teachers' reaction to her splinter, and she boasted proudly about how brave she was through it all. We could barely get her to eat dinner for all the talk of timber.

But as the night wound down and her bedtime drew near, my husband and I informed her that we would have to take out the splinter.

Her big saucer eyes blinked at us with confusion.

We explained that we didn't want the splinter to cause an infection. We couldn't leave it in her finger.

Blink. Blink.

Then we reached for the tweezers.

From that point forward, the most fascinating experience of our child's life turned into the most traumatic three days in our house.

Morning and night we pleaded with our screaming child. Begged her to just hold still for one minute so we could pluck the log from her thumb. Instead of relenting, she would wail dramatically and crawl up to the highest point on the nearest piece of furniture. We asked for help from her teachers, but they are not legally allowed to pull out splinters. They stood quite firm on this. And not a single teacher would bend to my attempts at backdoor bribery.

Finally, I had the bright idea to wait until our child was sleeping. We would sneak into her room with a flashlight and tweezers and gently extract the plank from her precious thumb. So that night, we bathed her, read her a story, put her to bed and waited.

When we heard her coherent talking shift into her sleep talking—a shift we are experts in discerning—we crept up the stairs. Jim carried the flashlight, and I had the traumatizing tongs at the ready. But as we picked up her hand and turned it toward the beam of light, we saw a pink, vacant slit in her thumb.

The splinter was gone.

It had worked its way out on its own.

This semester I taught four courses. And for one of the courses, Research Methods, I taught two sections. One was held during the day, the other at night. After the first few weeks of class, I began to see a startling difference in the way the two classes would respond to various assignments, lectures and tests. One section was better at presentations; the other had higher exam scores. One was more laid back; the other more serious. One preferred group projects; the other wanted to work independently.

I felt as if I was conducting a research experiment between two test groups.

The most notable difference between the two sections came during their final project. They had to use the almighty scientific method to form and test a hypothesis on themselves. For this, they needed to identify a problem in their lives—study habits, stress levels, social media addiction, etc.—and determine an intervention that could alleviate it.

Students had to meticulously track numerous variables for a week, then impose the intervention on themselves, and then track their progress for another week. They had to statistically analyze all the quantitative and qualitative data, then write up and graphically illustrate the findings.

I urged students to think about something in their lives they wanted to change. Give thought to a behavior or habit they felt was an obstacle to overcome. Allow this project to be a great excuse to improve their lives.

Both classes seemed skeptical. And hesitant.

Due to the personal nature of the project, I decided that instead of individually presenting their findings with a formal presentation, we would instead sit in a circle and have a discussion about the triumphs, and failures, of their research.

It's my personal opinion that empirical research doesn't have enough open dialogue.

Or hugs.

On the last night of section one, the students sat in a large circle with reports and charts on their laps. Their strange, nervous energy had me wondering if the assignment was an epic failure.

A female student volunteered to speak first. She had experimented with reducing stress through daily meditation. She found that 20 minutes of meditation in the morning showed a statistically significant difference in her stress level scales. She even found that when controlling for the stress variable of Thanksgiving, meditation was still effective.

The next student also wanted to reduce stress and assumed that having an hour of downtime in the morning would help. She found it did. Not only did she feel less stressed, but she also saw a spike in her productivity, especially on the days she spent her downtime away from electronics. A third student wondered if his stress could be lowered if he listened to classical music for a set amount of time in the afternoon. His data was less conclusive, but the anecdotal evidence was promising.

Another student increased the amount of quality time he spent with his girlfriend in an attempt to reduce the stress on their relationship.

While he had mostly positive results, the girlfriend did not enjoy discovering, after the fact, that she was part of an experiment. One student went a week without any form of social media to see if it increased happiness. She had the most significant data to present, but warned that the withdrawal was difficult and relapse was inevitable.

On and on, student after student talked about the one small modification they made in an attempt to affect positive change in their lives. While most students had significant success with their experiment, a few didn't. Those who didn't have success were reflective. Perhaps they measured the wrong variables. Others bemoaned a lack of rigidity with the intervention. Some wondered if they computed their data incorrectly.

But despite all the differences in the outcomes, there was one constant among the night class—they almost all chose to affect their stress levels.

I tried to look at that as a coincidence and not a reflection on my course.

The next day's class alleviated my concerns. We gathered around in a circle in the sun-soaked classroom, and everyone seemed relaxed. Numerous students volunteered to speak first. The first student said she had incorporated 30 minutes of exercise to see if it helped her sleep quality. She found that she not only had a significant increase in sleep quality (as tracked by a sleep monitoring device under her pillow), but she also stopped having headaches and lost five pounds.

Another said she decided to stop watching television at night in an attempt to get better sleep. Not only did she find a statistically significant difference in her sleep quality, but she didn't need to use the alarm clock. Another tried reading 15 minutes at night to see if it improved her sleep. Not only did it improve her sleep significantly, but she also realized she's a Harry Potter fan.

Student after student spoke excitedly about their experiments. Again, most had success, and others wished they could tweak their intervention or track different variables.

But in the day class, almost every single student tackled the issue of sleep.

I knew that wasn't on me.

After a long semester of exploring the rich details of research design, I felt the students finally understood the importance of experimentation and the power of validated results. They seemed hopeful, eager, empowered.

I was proud of how creative and introspective the students were about their behaviors and the outcomes from their changes in them. Students seemed surprised at how easily their lives were improved and appreciated having hard data to substantiate their improvements.

Was it possible that I not only showed them the importance of research by personalizing it, but did I also help everyone improve their lives?

Assuming I had indeed, I posed the same final question to each group of 20: Did they continue with the intervention after the assignment was over?

And in both classes, heads lowered.

Most everyone had immediately stopped their interventions and resumed their behaviors as normal.

The morning after my daughter's splinter had magically worked its way out by itself, we awoke to the sound of her excited screams.

"It's out! It's out!" she exclaimed, running around her room with her thumb triumphantly thrust skyward.

We danced around with her, excited for her victory. And even more excited that that portion of our life—the one in which we pleaded with a screaming child in an attempt to reduce the chance of infection while promising her candy corn for letting us help her—was over.

And it happened all on its own.

Reflecting on my two classes' individual research projects, I'm able to draw one substantial conclusion.

Change cannot be forced.

It can be feared. It can be embraced.

But not forced.

I suppose if my students really wanted to change a habit in their lives, they would. If they wanted to be on Facebook less, they'd log off. If they wanted better sleep, they'd get it. If they wanted a better relationship, they'd have it.

Because bad habits and negative behaviors are like menacing obstructions buried deep beneath the skin. At some point, it needs to be removed. And there's plenty of research that points to the most probable outcome:

It will work itself out on its own.

Vivid Imagination

Our three-year-old daughter has an imaginary friend. One day, while playing in the park with her father, Lowery looked up and out into the open space beyond the swings, pointed with vigor and yelled, "Daddy! There's Chasey Boom!"

Perplexed, my husband asked all the important questions about Chasey Boom to discover that he was a pink dog that drove a red car and had, apparently, come to the park that day to swing.

That night, when our child was tucked in her bed with her stuffed bear, her doll, and what is apparently a large, pink canine, we did an extensive Google search for the term "Chasey Boom." We were surprised to find this is not a character in a book, it is not an irritating television show on *Nick Jr.*, and it is not a proprietary name of a trendy new toy.

Nope.

Chasey Boom is all Lowery.

For the past six months we've observed our child's interaction with Chasey Boom and learned a great deal about him. For starters, Chasey Boom's hair turns brown at night, but is pink again by sun up. He is scared of spiders, loves to swing really high, and enjoys bath time. He's shy, but funny. Thin, but a big eater. And, he has seemingly sired all the stuffed animals in my child's toy chest, with the exception of the fuzzy giraffe, which Lowery claims "is a stray we took in."

Chasey Boom is not a family pet, however. Only Lowery has control. Jim and I lack the ability to add to her character's behavior. If we are trying to get her in the car and say something like, "Hurry up, Lowery! Chasey Boom is waiting!" she will stop and say, "That can't be. He's at the gym."

Lowery herself is an extremely layered character.

While she is willful and independent, she still responds to reason and discipline. While she's outgoing and fearless, she has her moments of timidity. She likes to be the center of attention, but she's extremely empathetic. She's active, but not hyper. She's verbal, but not bratty. Brilliant, but funny. Happy, but not easy going.

To me, she is magical.

Lowery's influence over me is substantial. From the moment I gave birth to her, Lowery has evoked in me an extremely strong reaction: she elicits energy. Often, this is positive. Any time I am near her, or sometimes just thinking of her, my heart races. I feel a flutter in my chest. This child excites, energizes and emboldens me more than any other person in my life.

I feed off her energy and charisma.

Energy, however, can manifest itself in negative ways as well. While my eldest does bring spirit and sparkle into my life, she also brings agitation and tension.

Lowery is insatiable at times. She's particular. And demanding. While she's always upbeat and happy, she's rarely satisfied. An afternoon with my child can be exciting and electrifying; it can also be challenging and unsettling.

She began talking at eight months of age. While her verbal skills are certainly remarkable, they are also extremely grating. From the moment she wakes up, our child is talking. We have to force her to stop just to take a bite to eat. She asks question after question and demands thoughtful responses. As the day wears on, the constant murmur of my child's sweet voice becomes akin to a small gnat buzzing in one's ear.

So by Sunday night, after two full days of hearing every single emotion, thought, sight, sound and taste my child has experienced, I can barely find the will to throw her in bed and say the words I've been longing to say all day: "It's quiet time now."

And even then, she talks in her sleep.
I appreciate that I always know what is going on with my child. Like me, she can only cope with emotions by vocalizing them. But with

Lowery, there is no down time. There's no deep breath. There's no quiet moment. Even though she can concentrate intently on certain activities, like painting or puzzles, she still narrates everything she's doing and demands you take part in the imagery.

So while my eldest child can pump me full of energy and excitement, she gives me no time to absorb it. Instead, she turns to me, extends her arm and, with the flick of her wrists says "Come on!" without realizing I need a moment to digest my feelings. Rest my feet. Shut my mouth. Empty my bladder.

Our younger daughter, London, on the other hand, is unflappable. She is expressive, but relaxed. She's vocal with her infant language. She's animated, but calm. She is a heavy sleeper, a great eater, a gentle crier, and she's easy to satisfy.

To me, she is mystical.

London's influence over me is significant. She evokes in me a powerful reaction: she conjures calmness. While Lowery energizes me in various ways, London instantly soothes me. To look at London, to hold her, to be near her, I find myself relaxed, comforted and at ease. This child assures me more than any person in my life. I appreciate her quietude and am enchanted by her serenity.

Within the first few weeks of London's life, I felt the energy in myself shift. Though the darkest period of the postpartum depression I experienced with Lowery only lasted six months, it wasn't until I held London for the first time that I truly felt it disappear. The relief of that heaviness—that anxiety that I had unknowingly still been carrying—was monumental.

The shift in myself and the ease with which I could satisfy my newborn had me convinced there was an enormous medical problem. I made an appointment with our children's pediatrician and had her give our newborn a thorough examination, after which she concluded that London was a happy, healthy and beautiful child. I refused her diagnosis. "What explains why she sleeps so well and is so damn calm?" I asked. The doctor laughed at my question, but then assured me that the only thing I was experiencing with London was luck.

Since the birth of my first child, and the unending anxiety that followed, I was suddenly aware of the substantial amount of tension I've carried around. It didn't occur to me, until I left the office with my youngest baby's clean bill of health, that I had been holding my breath for three years.

And, for the first time, I felt myself finally relax into motherhood.

Lowery *made* me a mother. Not just because of a technicality, but because the last three years have been an ongoing battle between the two of us. She's demanded my attention, challenged my self-esteem, battled my ambitions and held a mirror up to me by embodying so many of my personality traits.

She made me *earn* the title.

And London taught me to enjoy the moments I once found so unnerving. To calm myself by watching her example. To recognize the serenity I possess by reminding me what it looks like.

She made me *love* the title.

And then there's Chasey Boom. A character created deep in the recesses of my firstborn's vivid imagination. A character for whom we have to save a seat at the dinner table. A character whose hair I've had to brush alongside Lowery's in the morning. A character I've kissed goodnight for the last six months. A character who has served as my child's scapegoat for many small crimes.

It is not lost on me that Chasey Boom came to life during my pregnancy with London. Which is why I give Chasey Boom most of the credit for Lowery's mature acceptance of, and graceful transition into, sisterhood.

It's as if Lowery, a person who lives her life excitedly outward, had to search inward for something that would give her exactly what she needed to address an emotional ache that couldn't be soothed by me or her father.

She needed someone very specific, someone magical and mystical, to round out her needs. To challenge her way of being. To accept her and all her energetic ways. And to help her cope when energy fails her.

I understand and appreciate her motives. I, too, created a couple of creatures I assumed might influence me in beautiful and wonderful ways.

But this is so much more than I ever imagined.

Act II

Light opens on a dorm room. Two young women sit in the room; one on the bed, cross-legged, the other on the floor with her back against the wall. The room is fairly neat and orderly. An easel in the corner props up an unfinished painting. There is the subtle sound of laughter.

Older sister: [*laughter subsiding*]…and I said, "Okay, then, perhaps a second date isn't a good idea."

Younger sister: Oof. That's rough.

Older sister: It's fine, really. I mean, just because we sat next to each other in studio for two years doesn't mean we have to get married and have babies.

Younger sister: Yeah, I know. But you really liked him.

Older sister: I did. I mean, I *think* I did. [*opens a bag of chips and takes a few*] Actually, I was more turned on by his paintings than by him.

Younger sister: [*laughs*] Well, then hang one of them on your wall and move on.

Older sister: I intend to. [*passes bag of chips*] What do you want to do tonight?

Younger sister: [*shrugs*] Whatever. I'm easy to please.

Older sister: I know that. That's why you are Mom's favorite.

Younger sister: Oh whatever, she's miserable without you at home.

Older sister: I figured it would be a vacation for her.

Younger sister: [*eats chips*] Nope. I caught her crying in the bathroom the other day.

Older sister: And let me guess. She apologized.

Both girls laugh a bit and then turn quiet.

Older sister: That woman. [*shakes head*] Never met a person so in touch with her emotions and yet so apologetic for showing them.

Younger sister: I know.

Older sister: [*rolls eyes*] I miss her.

Younger sister: So call her.

Older sister: I will. It's just been busy with classes. [*pauses*] And What's-His-Name.

Younger sister: You mean What's-His-Name's paintings?

Older sister: [*laughs, tucks a curl behind her ears*] Yes.

They are both quiet. Younger sister eats her chips.
Older sister lies looking at the ceiling.

Younger sister: I'm not here because she sent me, you know.

Older sister: Why would I think otherwise?

Younger sister: You just seemed surprised when I wanted to visit.

Older sister: Well, spring break in a dorm isn't exactly Cancun. You're a senior. Shouldn't you be on a beach with your friends?

Younger sister: [*hangs head, pauses*] You're my best friend.

Older sister: Well, you're mine. [*sits up*] Are you crying?

Younger sister: [*sniffling*] It's just so hard being home without you. The dynamic is so different.

Older sister: It's been two years. Why is it a problem now? Because of Dad?

Younger sister: I dunno. I guess.

Older sister: Oh man...Am I not doing enough? Tell me. How can I help?

Younger sister: It's just not the four of us anymore. [*pauses*] You know you are the sun. We were all just orbiting.

Older sister: Don't confuse me with mom.

Younger sister: Stop.

Older sister: Oh come on, I caused as many problems as I solved.

Younger sister: [*sniffs and giggles*] *That's* putting it mildly.

Older sister: [*throws pillow at younger sister*] You'll be out of there next year.

Younger sister: Yes, on the other side of the country!

Older sister: I'm jealous. At least there's sun over there.

Younger sister: [*dabbing eyes*] I'm just scared.

Older sister: I completely understand. My freshman year was the worst. Remember when mom had to come stay with me for a week that first semester? I was losing hair in the shower!

Younger sister: Mom would do anything to save your hair.

Older sister: [*laughs, tugs and releases a curl*] I know.

Younger sister: She was really worried when she came back.

Older sister: [*picking at nails*] It was rough.

Younger sister: I wish you would have told me.

Older sister: I know. But you didn't need that on you.

Younger sister: Still…

Older sister: Besides, that stuff is really Mom's terrain.

Younger sister: I know she felt guilty about how stressed you got.

Older sister: It wasn't really her so much. It was the pressure of *everything.* The scholarship. The prestige of this school. The expectations on me. [*looks off*] I froze. I couldn't paint. I couldn't even eat.

Younger sister: She said she told you to give it up if you wanted. I couldn't believe it.

Older sister: I know, right? [*smiles*] Surprised me too. But she gets it. She understands the pressure. And she made it clear that if I didn't love it, it was going to be a miserable life.

Younger sister: Was that the problem? You started hating it?

Older sister: Not hating it. Just resenting it. I didn't want it to define me.

Younger sister: No wonder Mom understood…

Older sister: [*smirks*] Yep. That woman hates to be defined. Of course then *we* know the other extreme is being all over the place…

Younger sister: She seems okay with that.

Older sister: Downright proud.

Younger sister: Painting could never define you. [*pauses*] Only your hair does.

Older sister: Bitch.

Younger sister: [*laughs*] So? Do you still love painting?

Older sister: Oh yeah. I mean, I guess I didn't account for having to produce constantly. Consistently. It's not like it was when I was at home. But yeah, I love it.

Younger sister: So much so you fall in love with paintings instead of people.

Older sister: [*laughs*]. Exactly.

Younger sister: And now? I mean the fellowship…And your exhibition…excited or stressed?

Older sister: Both. [*shrugs*] But I think that's how it's supposed to be.

Younger sister: Well I am excited for you.

Older sister: Thanks. I mean, a passion has certainly been turned into work, but I'm still having fun. And Paris will be an amazing adventure.

Younger sister: Mom and Dad are really excited for the trip.

Older sister: Actually, I'm really glad you all are coming over.

Younger sister: Well yeah. It's not exactly a selfless endeavor. It's all we talk about over dinner every night.

Older sister: Oh, yeah. Family dinners by yourself. That *is* rough.

Younger sister: Oh [*swats hand*] it's okay.

Older sister: It will be nice to all be together. I kinda miss family dinners.

Younger sister: Family dinner in Paris!

Older sister: Exactly! And if I have another nervous breakdown, at least you all will be there.

Younger sister: Mom's at the ready.

Older sister: [*pauses*] I hate that I only feel really close to her when I'm in desperate need.

Younger sister: That's not true. You guys have a great relationship. [*bites at thumbnail*] I've always been kinda jealous of it.

Older sister: What!? That's ridiculous. We bitch at each other *constantly*. Besides, she's always preferred you.

Younger sister: No. She just loves that I'm so much like Dad. You know Mom needs us to ballast her a bit.

Older sister: Yeah. She and I are just too much alike.

Younger sister: Dad and I are always holding our breath [*winks*].

Older sister: He's the one I really miss.

Younger sister: Yeah. I know you do.

Older sister: How is he?

Younger sister: Oh, caught up in worrying about Mom.

Older sister: Status quo.

Younger sister: I mean, she's not moping around or anything.

Older sister: She never does.

Younger sister: But, you know. It's been an adjustment for all of us.

Older sister: Well, we'll always have Paris.

Phone rings. Younger sister answers it. Talking is muted while music plays. Older sister sits down at desk to fix her hair.

Older sister: All okay?

Younger sister: Yes. Just Mom checking that I made it safely. She's headed into a meeting and is going to call you after.

Older sister: Okay. Well, until then, what do you want to do?

Younger sister: I kinda like this. Feels like when we were kids and would sneak into each other's room at night.

Older sister: [*laughs*] So, Dad told me about your award.

Younger sister: [*rolls eyes*] He's so proud.

Older sister: He's proud when we blink.

Younger sister: I have to go to some dinner and accept it. Mom's beside herself, of course.

Older sister: You want me to come home for it?

Younger sister: No, no. It's not that big a deal. Everyone on the project is technically getting it. I mean, I think the trophy will stay in the case at school. Besides, it's a *science* award.

Older sister: Hey! I can do science. I took chem in high school.

Younger sister: Yes, covered in paint and barely squeaking by.

Older sister: Well, I'm excited for you. Even though you will have a miserable life as a scientist rather than as an artist.

Younger sister: It's a cleaner profession...

Older sister: There you go. Silver lining.

Younger sister: [*pauses, looking down at hands*] And, just so you know, I broke up with him.

Older sister: Oh! Why didn't you call me? [*moves down next to her and puts her arm around her*] Are you okay?

Younger sister: Yeah, I guess. I mean, I'm moving half way across the country in August. And, I dunno, it just didn't feel like I was experiencing the first love everyone talks about.

Older sister: Even though...

Younger sister: Yes. Even though.

Older sister: Are you okay about all that?

Younger sister: Yeah. I mean, it was a nice experience. We were careful. He was nice. It just wasn't a big deal, really.

Older sister: Well, maybe that's the problem.

Younger sister: Yeah, maybe.

Older sister: Well, take him as a beautiful experience. A great first who actually treated you well. [*looks off*] Not everyone can say that.

Younger sister: I know. [*squeezes her sister's hand*] He's great. And smart. [*pauses*] But I'm really excited about the idea of making this trek solo.

Older sister: You and your treks. Me and my paintings. Will we ever find love?

Younger sister: No joke.

Older sister: I think what you are doing is incredibly courageous. I mean, look at me. I fell apart the second I left home. And you? You are peeling people off of you so you aren't slowed down.

Younger sister: And that's good?

Older sister: I think so. Yes.

Younger sister: I don't know.

Older sister: I know what will help [*slaps her sister's leg*]. Let's smoke a little and then head to the movie on the lawn. We'll meet up with the usual suspects.

Younger sister: [*shrugs*] Sure. Sounds great.

The older sister pulls out a joint. They smoke it silently for a few minutes.

Older sister: So how's Dad? Really.

Younger sister: [*nodding, mouth full of smoke, exhales*] Good. Honestly. He's gaining weight back. Acts fine.

Older sister: Mom calming down?

Younger sister: Yeah. It was a lot. Especially without you home. But honestly, everything seems to have resolved itself. His doctor seems confident.

Older sister: I can't talk about this.

Younger sister: I know. I'm sorry.

Older sister: No, it's just, to me Dad is…[*hangs head*]

Younger sister: [*puts arm around her, puts head on her shoulder*] I know.

Older sister: [*takes long drag*] Okay. This is killing my buzz. Let's play the game.

Younger sister: [*gets up automatically and positions herself cross-legged in front of older sister*] Okay. Most recent nightmare?

Older sister: Oh! Just two nights ago. The one with the dog again. Though this time I woke up before it bit me.

Younger sister: Dude, see a shrink. Your turn.

Older sister: Biggest regret in the last month?

Younger sister: Um…[*looks at her pointedly*]

Older sister: Right. Your turn.

Younger sister: Best you thought you looked this past year?

Older sister: My date last night. What a waste. [*takes a drag*] Okay, most embarrassing moment this year?

Younger sister: I ran smack into that glass door. That one by the library.

Older sister: Who hasn't?! Remember when the librarian broke her nose on it?

Both girls laugh.

Younger sister: Favorite thing you've read this month?

Older sister: You'll just roll your eyes if I say the *New Yorker* piece on Armin Boehm.

Younger sister: Yep. Majorly.

Older sister: You'd rather me say Mom's latest.

Younger sister: Oh shut up.

Older sister: Best meal you've had today?

Younger sister: Those chips. Best lay?

Older sister: What a long list I have to choose from!

Younger sister: So then *not* the poetry guy from freshman year?

Older sister: Sure. [*laughs*] He'll do. Favorite book of all time?

Younger sister: *A Brief History of Time.* Thing you hate most about yourself?

Older sister: [*takes drag, thinks a bit*] Mmm…

Younger sister: You know the rules, no thinking!

Older sister: Okay, okay…Uh, my inability to be satisfied.

Younger sister: Poor Mr. Poetry.

Both laugh.

Older sister: Mom or Dad?

Younger sister: Mom. You?

Older sister: [*pauses one beat*] Dad.

Younger sister: Have you noticed that changes almost every time we play this?

Older sister: [*shrugs*] What's your biggest fear in life?

Younger sister: Um…[*pauses*]

Older sister: No thinking!

Younger sister: Uh…not being happy. Same question.

Older sister: Failing.

Younger sister: What have you ever failed at?

Older sister: [*inhales, holds smoke*] Chemistry.

Younger sister: [*laughs*] Whatever.

Older sister: When have you ever been unhappy?

Younger sister: I fear loneliness. Seems most unhappy people are that way because they are lonely.

Silent smoking.

Older sister: I love that you're here.

Younger sister: [*inhales, pauses*] Me too.

Older sister: Mom would love this.

Younger sister: She would? [*takes a drag pointedly*]

Older sister: I mean us just sitting in a room talking. She loved when we did that at home.

Younger sister: Yeah. [*exhales smoke slowly*] Guess we all miss it.

Girls sit silently, passing the joint back and forth.

Older sister: You'll never be lonely. You've got me.

Younger sister: [*pauses*] And you're gonna be a success. [*passes the joint to her*] It's all you know how to be.

Lights fade, smoke rises.

END SCENE

Mother of Invention

Parenting often feels like a constant cycle of trial and error. And often those trials don't feel particularly productive. There are lost causes, like trying to find matching pairs of toddler socks. There are upheavals, like a newborn's sleeping patterns. There are outright forfeits, like handing over your iPhone in the grocery store line to stave off your toddler's meltdown. But strife is also extremely fertile ground.

Ripe for innovation.

So long as the parent can be patient and wait. Because somewhere, amidst all the failures, a genius breakthrough is able to bubble up to the surface and change your life forever.

Stair Basket

Growing up, my best friend Kate lived in a two-story house. This meant that—unlike my own family's small one-story farmhouse— she had stairs. As if that weren't fascinating enough, she also had a stair basket. This was not just any basket. This was a basket that takes on the shape of stairs. A step-patterned profile that can sit atop two steps simultaneously.

The basket at my friend's house kept the stairs free of clutter, allowing everyone to put in various items that actually needed to go upstairs but were not worth a separate trip.

Last Christmas, my mother asked me for some gift ideas, so I mentioned the special stair-shaped basket. Now that Jim and I had a staircase of our own, I longed for an oddly shaped basket to place on it. Christmas morning she gifted me with an irregularly shaped basket—unwrapped, because, come on, how would you? So happy was I finally to have both a staircase and a basket to put on it. I felt unstoppable.

And yet, for months, I couldn't figure out its purpose. At first I put magazines in it. But magazines are really only needed on nightstands and toilet tanks, so that idea was scrapped. I tried putting throw blankets in the basket, but because we only use blankets on the couch, that's typically where they stay. I tried putting my purse in it when I came through the door, but frankly it just looked stupid having a bag inside a basket. Week after week, the basket contents changed until there was an odd month or so when nothing was in it at all. It just sat vacant on the stairs. Amazing, but empty.

But then one day, one magical day I shall never forget, my oldest child took off her shoes after school and left them on the stairs. They were muddy and in the way, so I, in a fit of rage, scooped them up and slammed them into the basket as I walked up the stairs. As I ascended, I felt my anger replaced with something far bigger: a revelation. When I reached the top of the stairs, I practically shouted out in excitement. Shoes! The basket could be for my three-year-old's tiny, muddy, scattered everywhere, can-never-find-the-mate, shoes! I ran into her bedroom and gathered up every pair she owned. I raced back down the stairs and yelped when I realized all eight pairs fit perfectly into the stair basket.

The next morning, without any prompting from me, my child came down the stairs and dug through the basket to find her favorite pair of sparkly TOMS. That evening, when she came through the door, dirty and muddy, she took off her shoes and threw them in the basket.

I had never loved her more.

We embraced in the way veterans embrace their loved ones upon returning home from war. We spun around the living room joyfully realizing that both of our problems were solved by this solitary piece of woven wonder.

Hair Purse

My three-year-old has curly hair. This statement means something to people who have curly hair, or to mothers with children who have curly hair. And if you are neither of these, you probably know someone with curly hair, or perhaps know of someone who knows of someone with curly hair. Send them loving thoughts.

My own hair, which is straight, can be easily brushed and pulled back into a ponytail with little to no whining and not a drop of product. But, as I've learned, curly-haired people are not afforded the same luxuries.

As an intentional strategy on my part, I give my child freedom over her hair. This means that every morning she gets to decide how she wants to wear it (this does not apply on picture day, national holidays or her birthday). She can choose a ponytail, pigtails, barrettes, a headband, or down and curly. For a while she demanded the Elsa braid from *Frozen*, which is improbable given her short, spiraled hair. Sometimes she demands to wear a hat, but never a stylish hat. A ski cap or an old birthday party hat. But, with my styling abilities being the only limits, she gets full follicle freedom.

Each morning she chooses a different hairstyle, which requires accoutrements scattered around the house. The spray bottle is always in the laundry room. The hair gel stays in the bathroom. The hair ties, clips, bows and headbands stay in Lowery's room on her dresser. And the brush and comb are usually in places we fail to look as we are hurrying in the morning.

For her third birthday, Lowery was gifted with a little canvas purse with two leather handles. It's adorable, and she loves carrying it around. She likes to fill it with things a gal-about-town would need, like raisins and socks. But one day, after I had pulled her hair up in two glorious pigtails with sparkly bows and a pink clip, I asked her to pick up the living room before we left for school. Lowery looked at everything strewn on the couch—hair bows, gel, a water bottle, detangler, a comb and a brush—gathered them all up, took them over to the canvas purse, and dumped them in.

"Let's hang this with the coats!" she declared.

I shrugged, happy she was helping pick up, and hung the bag of hair products on the coat rack next to her rain jacket and my umbrella. The very moment I put the bag on the hook, my life forever changed.

For a year I had tried different approaches to our morning routine. Getting her ready in the upstairs bathroom. Fixing her hair in her bedroom. Wrestling her to the ground to put in a sparkly clip. Doing her hair before she even got out of bed in the morning. But no matter the process I tried to implement, we always ended up doing her hair by the front door right before she left for school. And this was always stressful because I was running around looking for clips and combs.

But now, there by the door hangs a bag of all of Lowery's hair products. So as we walk out of the house, I can easily access everything I need to get Lowery's day started off right: perfectly coiffed.

Tandem Carts

There are few activities I hate more than grocery shopping. I find it long and boring and expensive, and I never get home with everything I need. Jim is more than happy to go for me, and usually does, but I still have to write out an extremely detailed grocery list. I can never decide if I should go during the week after work when I'm tired, but without the kids. Or on the weekends, when I have more energy, but also have the children. If I go with the kids, I usually come home in such a state of depression, or exhaustion, that I refuse to cook anything I bought.

But one Saturday, a few weeks back, Jim and I needed diapers and wipes and a variety of foods to nourish our children. While we have done many configurations of grocery shopping, we'd never gone together with both children.

When we reached for a cart, our three-year-old demanded to ride in one. Because we had the infant in her carrier, there simply wasn't room for both children and groceries. Jim and I looked at each other blankly.

"I guess I could just get a cart by myself and Lowery could ride in that…" Jim shrugged.

"Okay…" I said, unaware of how my life was about to dramatically change.

So with London safely resting in her carrier in my cart, and Lowery in the seat of Jim's cart, we began rolling one after the other into the store. And I swear a fluorescent light came on above me.

"Do you think you could take your cart and go get toilet paper?" I asked Jim.

As he left, I gathered up everything we needed in the produce section and then texted Jim to get eggs and butter. I went off in search of meat and bread. After a bit, we saw each other across the store and he yelled down the aisle: "MILK?"

"YES!" I shouted. "I'LL GET RICE!"

Texts whirled back and forth:

> Got diapers
>
> > Got chicken
>
> Pancake mix?
>
> > Yes. I'll get syrup
>
> I'll get diaper rash cream
>
> > Oh no…she has a rash?
>
> Ketchup?
>
> > Yes. And mayo too.
>
> This is fun.
>
> > You're fun.
>
> Stop flirting. Get bagels.

On and on until we finally met at the front of the store with two carts full of food. And children. We looked at each other proudly. We had done it. We had figured it out. We had invented the smartest, easiest, quickest, most productive and relaxing way to grocery shop with children. We embraced each other passionately. A tear rolled down my cheek. Swollen with pride and elation, we wheeled our carts one after the other into the checkout lane.

"We are together!" I exclaimed to the checkout lady.

She looked up and over her half glasses. Peered at my cart and then at Jim's. And I could tell by the expression on her face that what she was seeing was nothing new.

Becoming a parent warrants ingenuity. But for the first few years of parenting, everything felt like a loss. A loss of sleep. Loss of time. Loss of privacy. Loss of identity. But eventually, we began to have some victories. We began to see our lives adjust and accommodate our children. And when we are open to it, we can be innovative if we patiently allow circumstances to take over.

Because necessity truly is the mother of invention.

So long as she mates with Father Time.

Fear Itself

My three-year-old daughter is obsessed with dogs. She is also terrified of them.

This creates a bit of a problem, as well as confusion, considering we have a pet dog.

Lowery's first word was "dog." As an infant, she would only invest in books with a dog as a prominent character. She preferred her stuffed dogs over dolls. And she insisted on wearing a shirt with a dog in glasses on the front over and over and over.

And yet, she fears our dog.

The dog is a ten-pound pug, a breed which ranks among the top of those great for—and with—children. Our pug, a fawn colored eight-year-old named Izzy, is a placid, affectionate and gentle dog who never barks. She doesn't have the best vision, so she's not prone to run wildly about the house. She is trained not to jump on furniture. And she sleeps a majority of her day.

But none of this qualifying information pacifies our child.

She still fears the skillet-faced creature.

Her fear manifests itself in a fairly subtle way. If she sees Izzy walking through a room, she quietly shifts out of her path. If Izzy is under the couch chewing on a bone, Lowery is sitting on the chair opposite the couch. She sits cross-legged at the dinner table so Izzy won't sniff her feet.

Our younger child will sit on the floor happily tugging at the pug's fat rolls, while our three-year-old sits on the coffee table with her feet tucked under her.

Now, if the baby gate is erected in the kitchen, to keep the pug corralled while I vacuum, Lowery will sit at the gate and talk and sing to her.

But she won't touch her.

Lowery's fear is an inconvenience, it's a nuisance and, frankly, it's ridiculous.

We've tried every trick in every child psychology book. We've awarded good behaviors, like the time she actually let Izzy lick her hand. We've ignored bad behaviors, like the time she burst out crying because the pug sneezed on her.

In one traumatizing immersion therapy session, we let our pug outside and then made Lowery stand outside alone with her. But then the neighbors called about all the blood-curdling screams, so we had to stop for the day.

There's no adequate way to explain the frustration Jim and I feel over this. Every day is a battle of wills between our daughter and our pug. We are constantly trying to make the two opposing forces live together in harmony.

And while we find our daughter's fear annoying and unfounded, we do recognize true fear when we see it.

True fear is subtle. Quiet. And is born out of those situations we can't, or won't, avoid.

A friend of mine insists his biggest fear in the world is to be eaten by sharks. I find this ridiculous, because it's fairly easy to avoid them.

Especially in Oklahoma.

Another friend of mine has an acute fear of drowning. Easy enough: don't swim. My sister fears scorpions. But she's never once come within stinging range of one. A student of mine said he fears bungie jumping. You can imagine my empathy.

True fear can't be of the creatures or situations we can easily avoid. Why would someone ever fear being buried alive? What are you doing, running deals for the mafia?

No, there is a special type of fear. The fear that we live with every day.

For example, I fear falling down stairs. This may seem small. But it's real.

I live in a house with stairs. I work in an office with stairs. I shop in stores with stairs. And I generally like to move upward in life.

While I've never experienced a bad fall, I constantly fear one is coming. I don't have great balance. I have a weak hip that I fear re-injuring. And I'm never quite sure what I'd do with my hands. I'm fairly certain I would try to protect my face instead of bracing my fall.

I fear falling and breaking my front teeth. I fear tripping down a flight while holding my infant. I fear I'll fall at work while wearing a dress and I'll roll hand over feet with my skirt high above my undies, giving all those in the stairwell a show. And concrete stairs? Forget it.

Stairs aren't all I fear, of course.

I also fear that I will burn my house down by leaving on my hair straightener. Now, one might suggest I stop using a flat iron to avoid the issue. Okay. Then I'll fear leaving my curling iron on. Stop using that? Okay, now my hot rollers have set the house ablaze.

My husband, however, has a bigger looming fear he carries with him every day. He first told me his as part of a trust exercise during our premarital counseling classes. He looked at me earnestly, took a deep breath and confessed his deepest fear: failure.

I laughed out loud. In his face. Really hard.

His hurt look should have evoked an apology from me. But I kept going.

"Failure!?" I snorted.

"Yeah..." he sighed, looking like he was questioning his decision to marry me.

"Failure at what?"

"Everything."

"I just don't get that at all," I said, realizing I might make for a horrible spouse.

"That's because fear is the *only* emotion you never seem to feel."

And yet, this is the man who never hesitates when climbing or descending stairs. In fact, he does that super gloaty thing all tall people do: he takes them two at a time.

Jim's fear of failure, I've learned through the years, is not irrational. It's not from a place of insecurity. Or doubt. It's from a place of love. He fears failing in this life he's worked so hard to build. He fears failing as a father, failing as a spouse, a son, an employee. Essentially, he fears losing all the things he loves because of his own inability to maintain them.

So, perhaps I was wrong to laugh in his face.

But he's wrong about fear escaping me.

It's true I don't fear failure, but that's only because I'm too caught up in the high of *trying* new things to worry about the low of failing at them. But I fear all kinds of things that are not avoidable in the way sharks and shallow graves are.

I fear another traumatic car accident, but I have to drive a car every day. I fear anything happening to my children. I fear losing my parents. I fear ever losing my job. I fear disappointing my friends.

But I refuse the alternative: a life without these things I love.

So, just like my pug and my child, I have to find a way for two opposing forces to live together in myself.

Despite our frustration with Lowery's fear of dogs, we are proud of how hard she's trying. She never screams or cries about the dog. She rarely throws fits or is demanding about it. She talks about Izzy endlessly. She is genuinely worried when Izzy has to get her yearly shots. She colors pictures of her, she makes up songs about her and she constantly refers to Izzy as her "hairy sister."

But she's still living in fear of her.

So we are impressed by how hard she works every day to have her fear of Izzy, and her love for Izzy, coexist within herself.

Because essentially, her father and I are doing the same thing every day as parents. As spouses. As friends. As employees.

The reassuring moments, in which I know the fear is manageable, are in the mornings. The best part of my day is waking Lowery. She's always curled up under her blanket with just a tuft of matted hair poking out. I'll pull back the covers and stare at her for a while, my heart bursting with love and aching with fear. I'll brush the tangled mess of curls off her face and kiss her nose gently.

She'll startle and stretch. She'll smile knowing I'm close, but won't open her eyes.

"Is sister awake?" she'll always ask first.

"Yes," I'll say. "Downstairs waiting on you."

"Is it a school day?" she'll ask, eyes still closed.

"Yes."

"And where's Izzy?" Her eyes will open for the answer.

"At the bottom of the stairs."

And she will get up and reach for my hand as we walk together to the top of the stairs and look down to see the pug.

She'll squeeze my hand. I'll squeeze hers back. She'll look at Izzy. I'll look at the flight of stairs stretched before us. We'll both momentarily remember our fears. But we both know we can't escape them. So we walk toward them.

One step at a time.

Overreaching

W hen my husband was in high school, he asked his parents if he could go to New York City during winter break. They agreed, back in the days before cell phones and Giuliani's clean up of Times Square, to let Jim experience NYC all by himself.

The jury is still out on whether or not this decision makes my in-laws amazing parents or outright negligent, but off their teenage boy went to the Big Apple solo.

While there he stayed in a cheap motel in Yonkers and awoke early every morning to ride the bus into the city. He spent 12 hours each day walking the streets, eating at restaurants, attending plays and riding in taxis, before catching a late bus back to the suburb.

When Jim was a junior in college, he decided he wanted to attend film school. For a top film school, he needed to go to NYC or LA. Despite having grown up in small-town Oklahoma, despite having lived at home all through college, and despite having never been to the West Coast, Jim applied to USC and was accepted. And so, he set out to live and attend graduate school in the gang-ridden South Central area of Los Angeles.

There, living in the slums, Jim graduated top of his class with a Master of Fine Arts degree in film and television production. During his final semester, he went with some classmates to the ABC Studios lot for a guided tour of the stages. During the tour, he befriended a writers' assistant for *General Hospital*, and a few days later was offered an internship on the show. A few months following, the internship turned into a staff position, and he spent years helping write the show and even shared in two Emmys.

Later, having decided to leave behind the fast-paced and outrageously expensive life in LA, Jim moved back to Oklahoma to buy a house, find a wife and have some babies. But before he settled down, he saw an online ad seeking a television scriptwriter for the World Wrestling Federation (now the WWE). Or as Jim calls it, soap operas for sweaty men. Having long been a fan of professional wrestling (I know, I know), and with experience in long-form story telling, Jim applied for, and was given, the job.

So, despite having just bought a house in Oklahoma, he took off for Connecticut, at 6 feet tall and 130 pounds, to sit in a room full of 7-foot-tall, 350-pound professional wrestlers and draft their stories from week to week. At the time Jim was writing for two of the most famous wrestlers—Stone Cold Steve Austin and The Rock—for the highest rated cable show on TV: *Monday Night Raw*. There sat my slender, smart, sophisticated and soft-spoken husband—between hulking, ambitious and powerful men— pitching ideas of how they could poetically bash each other over the head with metal folding chairs.

In general, I have a level of unfounded confidence that gets me through most of the bigger challenges in life. But there are also moments of intimidation and insecurity in which I feel perhaps I've overreached my potential. Out-stretched my abilities.

When I was in high school, my parents insisted I enroll in advanced calculus. They had forced this on my sister and brother several years earlier, so I knew I probably wouldn't escape this absurdity. Thus, as a senior in high school, I was in class with 15 other students who I came to understand were not there because their parents demanded it, but because they had tested extremely well and earned their seat in the classroom.

Our calculus teacher, despite being among the greatest instructors I've ever had, did one truly traumatizing thing: she posted our grades on the wall. And while only our social security numbers identified us, there was only ever one grade lower than an A in the entire class. So not only did I feel like the idiot in the classroom, but now a large group of really smart people had my SSN.

It took years of self-love and therapy to see that, while I didn't make an A in advanced calculus, I also didn't do horribly. In fact, I finished that course with a B, and I have gone on to have a fairly normal and productive life.

When I studied abroad during college, I felt instantly I had overreached. Every part of leaving my home country to live for half a year in a foreign land—even an English-speaking one—was difficult. When our plane touched down in London that first day, I was full of enthusiasm and energy. But when we arrived on campus, my roommate and I were told our dorm room was not yet ready and to come back in a few hours.

She wandered off to buy a cell phone and some toiletries, leaving me to roam the city all alone on my first day in another country.

While I'd like to say that I went skipping through London drinking tea and looking for the Queen, I actually sat down on a park bench and cried. I was homesick and terrified. Lonely and afraid. And I was fairly certain that I could not survive six solid months in this strange land where cars drove on the other side of the road and it rained constantly.

While I now look back on my time studying abroad with nothing but warm feelings and pleasant memories, the first few weeks were brutal. I used my showers every morning to cry. The early days abroad had me truly believing I was pathetic. I had stretched out my arms for this amazing adventure and felt I couldn't quite grab hold of it.

But after I tackled the first month, I began to find my rhythm. I stopped crying in the shower and started drinking at the pub. I went with my roommates to plays on the West End, bars in SoHo and markets in Piccadilly. We started planning trips to France, Switzerland and Italy. Before the month was up, I dreaded returning to the States.

Recently I attended an academic conference focused on my field of study. There, the top researchers in the field gathered to share ideas, papers and teaching strategies. For three solid days I attended session after session in which highly accomplished scholars shared the newest and greatest research being conducted in the field.

Now, as junior faculty, I don't expect to know what these scholars know. I'm not being asked to present such sophisticated research at this stage in my career. But I will be expected to at some point. And so, with every session, I saw my future unfold and felt my skin break out in a sweat. Beyond that, I often feel a bit of a fraud when I'm teaching students who are in their 60s or when a student asks if

I'm old enough to have any experiences in the field. Despite graduating with the right degrees and securing a faculty position, I still feel my arms aren't long enough to envelop it all.

And don't get me started on how much I overreached when I became a mother. Even three years in, I feel a bit under qualified to raise these strong and beautiful girls.

The other night, while out to dinner, I asked Jim about his time in New York, LA and Connecticut. Mostly, I wanted to know how he was able to repeatedly put himself into situations in which he was clearly reaching beyond his potential. How did he manage to always extend his arms and grab the things that were just beyond his reach? And, more importantly, why did he never see himself as overreaching?

He shrugged.

"In high school, before I left for New York, I read something in a travel book about how to survive as a tourist in the city," he recalled. "Guess it just stuck with me."

"Oh?" I asked. "What did it say?"

"When you reach your destination, you've earned the right to be there."

The Final Act

Light opens on a bedroom. An older couple is packing a suitcase. Clothes are strewn about.

Wife: Is it supposed to snow there?

Husband: I can't imagine.

Wife: Better take clothes just in case.

Husband: Honey. Stop for a second.

Wife: [*rummaging through closet*] No. I want to make sure I have everything.

Husband: You do. Slow down. There's time.

Wife: We should change the flight up again.

Husband: If we did, it would only put us there a few hours earlier. We are leaving at 4 a.m. as it is.

Wife: I need to be there. I'm going out of my mind.

Husband: I know, but we will be there in less than 12 hours.

Wife: I should have gone up earlier.

Husband: When? The second she got pregnant?

Wife: Yes. [*folds a shirt*] Better than the week she's due.

Husband: We will get there in plenty of time.

Wife: When it comes to the girls, there is never enough time.

Husband: Lunny is there. She's got everything under control.

Wife: That's *my* job.

Husband: Darling, I need you to stay calm. You getting upset will upset Cakes.

Wife: [*looks at her husband a long time, eventually sits on the bed, hangs head*] I know. I know it will. I'm trying so hard not to upset her again.

Husband: [*comes to his wife's side, sits with her, holds her hand*] I didn't mean like that. That storm has passed. All I meant was that she has to focus on giving birth, and she needs to stay calm.

Wife: You're right. [*wipes eyes*] I just don't ever want to risk it.

Husband: I know, I know. [*strokes her hair*] It will never be like that again. I promise. Things are different between you two.

Wife: I never saw it coming the first time, so how the hell do I avoid it a second time?

Husband: [*pauses*] You can't. But I promise you, she's at a different place in her life.

Wife: [*wipes eyes and rises*] I don't have time to worry with that now. All I know is, I need to get to her. So, goose down parka?

Husband: I promise it is not going to snow.

Wife: I'll take it just in case.

Husband: Did you already get the medicine kit?

Wife: Yes. The doctor gave us extra pills so we can stay longer if need be.

Husband: Oh. I didn't know you had requested that.

Wife: Well, I don't know what to expect when we get up there. You remember what it's like when you have a baby for the first time.

Husband: Right.

Wife: And you are sure you feel up for flying? Because you can drive out later if you're worried…

Husband: I feel fine.

Wife: Okay, because I can always get my sister to—

Husband: Darling.

Wife: [*holds hand up*] Okay.

The couple continues to pack in silence.

Husband: I love you.

Wife: I love you more.

Husband: I know you're worried on a multitude of levels. But this is Cakes we are talking about. The girl is unstoppable.

Wife: I know…

Husband: And she has her sister with her. Those two navigated Pakistan for a month. They can do this.

Wife: I know…it's just…

Husband: What?

Wife: I just can't worry enough for her. I just lie awake every night going over all the things I know she's about to experience, and I'm so worried for her. And excited for her. And nervous. And scared. And thrilled. And sick to my stomach.

Husband: I know. But you didn't do it alone, remember? And neither will she.

Wife: [*laughs*] I know. [*pauses*] Thank god it's with him.

Husband: I'm so proud of the two of them.

Wife: Yes. She's the perfect version of herself with him.

Husband: They remind me of us back then.

Wife: Back then? What, are we old and awful now?

Husband: [*laughs*] Quite the contrary. You've gotten so beautiful I can barely breathe.

Wife: I'll call the doctor.

Husband: He knows he can't fix the strain you put on my heart.

Wife: Maybe we should split up. For your health.

Husband: I considered it. But a broken heart is no better than a weak one.

Wife: Fine. We'll stay together. But you know the risks.

Husband: Are you taking the baby blankets?

Wife: I was going to…

Husband: But?

Wife: I can't part with them…

Husband: Darling, the girls asked for them. Cakes wants to sew a new one from both of their blankets.

Wife: I know. [*points to velvet chair in the corner*] I have them out. It's just hard.

Husband: Take different blankets. They won't know the difference.

Wife: [*laughs*] Good thought. But you know how particular she is about these things. I have no choice.

Husband: There's strength in letting go.

Wife: I'm content being weak.

Husband: You've got an attic full of those girls. Their rooms are just like they were in high school. The walls are covered in Cakes' artwork.

Wife: Fine. They can have the blankets. But I'm keeping all the headbands.

Husband: I call that real growth.

> *Wife laughs. They come around the bed to embrace.*
> *They kiss lightly and resume packing.*

Husband: All is squared away on campus, right?

Wife: Yes. My first semester without a class in 30 years.

Husband: I can't believe that.

Wife: Boy I can.

Husband: [*smiles*] You okay leaving it behind for a few months?

Wife: Absolutely. You know my girls come first.

Husband: Of course I know that. But I also know how important your work is to you. [*pauses*] And I know what it means to leave it.

Wife: Retirement and sabbatical aren't exactly the same things.

Husband: Be glad for that.

Wife: Oh hush. You're having a blast.

Husband: I know, I know.

Wife: Besides, you're finally getting all that reading done.

Husband: Time enough at last!

Wife: What are you taking with you?

Husband: [*points to books on nightstand*] This stack.

Wife: All plays I assume?

Husband: You know it.

Wife: And my latest, right?

Husband: Top of the heap.

> *Wife goes to closet and fishes while*
> *Husband is at dresser going through drawers.*

Wife: When's the last time you talked to Cakes?

Husband: Yesterday. You can tell she's ready.

Wife: There's a difference between being ready and being tired of pregnancy.

Husband: Maybe that's what it is. The midwife is stopping by tomorrow morning to check her again.

Wife: [*sighs*] Okay.

Husband: Darling...

Wife: I can be worried about this birth.

Husband: Worried about it or critical of it?

Wife: She's giving birth in her fucking bedroom!

Husband: Yes, I know. This is the decision they've made and we're supporting them.

Wife: I understand the need to have a certain kind of birth. I understand the need to control the environment, but in this day and age…

Husband: It's out of our hands. All we can do is be there to help.

Wife: I know. [*pauses*] Honestly, I'm just grateful she wants me in the room.

Husband: A tradition lives on.

Wife: I just feel so close to her right now. And so grateful I've been part of this.

Husband: You were the first person she called when she got her test results. Even before her sister.

Wife: I know. [*pauses*] God those girls…

Husband: She'll be an amazing mother.

Wife: [*pauses*] I'm just remembering how very hard it is.

Husband: I know. But it might not be as hard a transition for her as it was for you.

Wife: I'm fearful she won't go back to work.

Husband: She's got people to manage the gallery for a while. Let her enjoy her time off. She can make that decision when she's ready.

Wife: [*bites thumbnail*] Well, I know better than to project onto her.

Husband: A tough lesson to learn.

Wife: It will be fine. She's healthy and strong and determined as hell. I'm mostly just upset that I won't know the gender of my first grandchild until he or she is born.

Husband: Oh? Were you wanting to knit a blanket and needed to know the yarn color?

Wife: [*laughs*] You never know.

Husband: You talk to Lunny this morning?

Wife: Of course.

Husband: And?

Wife: Being her usual self.

Husband: Calm and collected in the face of her sister's histrionics?

Wife: Pretty much. She only has a week off of work and she's worried her sister will need her longer.

Husband: That girl…

Wife: I know. She hasn't even told her about the grant. She doesn't want her worried about anything but the baby.

Husband: I can understand that.

Wife: She'll be over there for six months. Maybe eight.

Husband: Yes, but what an opportunity.

Wife: I know, but she's really conflicted now that she's going to have a niece. Or nephew. [*rolls eyes*] Dammit I wish I knew what kind of genitals this baby has!

Husband: Soon.

Wife: Anyway, she said she may not even go.

Husband: What?! Because of the baby? That's ridiculous.

Wife: No, I don't think it's because of the baby. Entirely.

Husband: Then what?

Wife: I don't know. I think she's tired of traveling. If you can believe that.

Husband: [*shrugs*] Most people have to wait until retirement to do the kind of traveling she's done in the last five years.

Wife: I think she wants to stand still for a while. And honestly, I think she's lonely. I think she wants what her sister has. Or at least a chance to put down some roots.

Husband: Well, I support her either way.

Wife: Me too.

Husband: I can't believe we are here.

Wife: In our bedroom?

Husband: In this phase of our life.

Wife: [*goes to husband and puts her arms around him*] Me either.

Husband: I never dreamed I'd make it this far.

Wife: Stop…

Husband: No, I don't mean my health. I mean, there was a time I thought I'd never even find someone. And now [*brings wife in for an embrace, rests his head on top of hers*], well, now I'm flying out to see my first born have her first born.

Wife: I know…

Couple embraces quietly.

Wife: [*breaks embrace*] Okay, softie. Enough of that.

Husband: [*clears throat*] Right.

Wife: Got underwear?

Husband: Check.

Wife: Toothpaste?

Husband: Roger.

Wife: Medicine?

Husband: Affirmative.

Wife: Baby gifts?

Husband: Yes.

Wife: Okay…well, I seem to be all packed up here.

Husband: I'm ready, just have to check us into our flight and we are—

Husband is interrupted by a ringing phone. Wife answers it.

Wife: Hi sweetie! [*pauses*] Okay. So, where is she now? [*pauses, turns to Husband and whispers*] This is Lunny. They are at the hospital with Cakes. [*back to phone*] Is the baby okay? [*long pause*] But the bleeding has stopped? [*pauses*] Is your sister okay? [*Husband and Wife both pace around the bedroom*] Hang on. [*turns to Husband*] She had some bleeding and some pain and they couldn't get a hold of her midwife. Lunny made them go to the hospital and it looks like there could have been a rupture of the placenta, but they caught it in time. They will do a C-section tomorrow. [*back to phone*] Sweetie, thank you for taking care of them. And for being you. You're a rock. Is your sister where she can talk? [*pauses*] Hi darling…are you okay? [*pauses*] Honey, I know. I know it isn't. But Cakes, you and the baby are safe and that's really what matters. [*pauses*] Honey. Honey, I know, calm down. Please calm down. I know this isn't at all how you planned it, but darling, I can promise you none of this will matter tomorrow. All that will matter is that you and the baby are safe. [*pauses*] Our plane lands at 8 a.m. [*pauses*] Well, see? I'll be there in plenty of time. [*pauses*] That's okay. Honey, I understand the circumstances. But I'll be in the waiting room and will be by your side the second you are out of surgery. [*pauses*] What? [*looks at Husband who is clearly wanting information. Wife still listening*] Oh honey—[*pauses*] Okay, okay, I understand. [*pauses*] I love you more. [*pauses*] We will see you tomorrow. Get some rest.

Wife lays down the phone and sits on the bed crying.

Husband: Tell me! What? What's happening!?!

Wife: [*sobbing*] She's—she's so upset. This isn't at all how she wanted this to go and she's so upset.

Husband: But she's okay, right? The baby's okay?

Wife: [*sobbing*] Yes. Everyone is safe and fine. The cesarean is tomorrow morning at 9 unless something happens between now and then.

Husband: [*sighs*] Okay. Well, at least she's being monitored and we have a plan.

Wife: That's not all.

Husband: What? What else?

Wife: The ER doctor didn't know she was trying to keep the gender a secret.

Husband: Oh no…

Wife: He blurted it out while going over her chart.

Husband: Dammit. So now she knows.

Wife: [*sobbing*] I feel horrible for her. She's feeling completely out of control.

Husband: I can imagine. [*punches pillow*] Dammit!

Wife: I should have gone out there earlier…

Husband: Wait. Did she tell you the gender?

Wife: [*sobbing*] Yes.

Husband: And…?

Wife: [*slowly gets sobbing under control, smiles slightly through tears*] It's a girl.

Lights fade as the couple embraces.

END SCENE

CURTAINS CLOSE

Tabling the Discussion

My three-year-old daughter is a shrewd negotiator.

One of her many schemes is to convince us to let her reserve something for later if we won't let her have it in the moment. She'll come to us and ask for a piece of candy. The answer is usually no. She'll nod respectfully but then ask for the same thing in a different way:

"Can I put a piece of candy on the table?"

When we ask why she wants to do this, she explains that perhaps later, maybe after dinner, it would be all right for her to have the piece. And if it is, the candy will be ready for her.

This is surprisingly effective.

At any given time in our house, the dining room table is littered with objects or treats over which my child is in current negotiations. And yet, by bedtime, the table is always magically cleared of clutter.

In my beginning years of teaching at the college level, I unknowingly developed a bad habit: I favored the male students. While this was completely unintentional, I came to the realization a few years in that I was constantly deferring to the men in my classes.

Now, in my own flimsy defense, there were many reasons why this was the case. For starters, during the first five years of teaching I was an adjunct and taught undergrads at night in a different town. Often, I was the only person in the entire building late at night with my 20 or so students. To some degree, both conscious and unconscious, I felt a tiny bit of fear as a young female with so many male students. One night in class, during a particularly heated debate about gun control in which two male students became verbally threatening, I actually had justification.

Aside from that, I've always gotten along really well with men. In the romantic comedy of life, I am continually type-cast as the protagonist's funny best friend. I was a friend to boys growing up. I was a friend to boys in college. And I worked better with men than with women in my first few jobs out of college. So, as an instructor, I naturally gave men the attention I'd always given them.

All of that is on me.

But, the other side is that the men naturally behaved differently in class. They talked louder. Interjected without fear. Effortlessly criticized my thoughts or the thoughts of their classmates. Blurted out without thought. And never struggled to speak their minds. This is an intimidating and powerful thing to watch from the perspective of the instructor. No wonder I favored them; they gave me something to favor.

And yet, the women in my class were consistently better writers, more effective public speakers, more thoughtful debaters and kinder classmates.

So when it finally occurred to me, on the long drive home one night after class, that I was more likely to pay attention to the men—because of fear, intimidation, interest and awe—I knew I had to change my ways.

The next class period I publicly apologized to the students. I spoke to everyone but only made eye contact with the women. I said that while I knew I had been fair in grading, perhaps I'd been too quick to defer to the louder, deeper voices in the class. And, from that day forward, I pledged to be the biggest advocate the women in the class ever had. I offered them private meetings, reference letters, job counseling, or to buy them a copy of *Lean In*. And then I challenged them to speak up. Sit on the front row. Interject more. And to not be overrun by the men in the class as I had been.

Everyone stared at me blankly.

After class that night I felt foolish. How arrogant of me to assume any of the female students needed my advice, let alone wanted it. Maybe my favoritism toward the men had been invisible to them. Did I just draw their attention to something they'd never even noticed? Did I offend the women? Alienate the men?

Yet the next day I received two emails, both from female students asking for letters of recommendation. A third asked for career advice. And a handful of others added me as a friend on Facebook.

Currently—having moved on from long commutes and late night classes to a full-time position with office hours—I find myself in very different terrain. And my relationship with my female students is quite different.

Teaching at the graduate level provides a very different student dynamic than the undergraduates to which I'd grown accustomed. For one thing, women don't struggle in class to compete with the men. They contribute equally. I don't find myself deferring to the male voices, as they never overpower a woman's. Happily, my female and male students are equal in the classroom. Both genders interject without fear. Challenge each other. Both are strong writers, good speakers and kind to each other.

While there isn't much difference between my male and female students academically at the graduate level, there absolutely is at the personal level. My female students are struggling with a host of concerns that my male students either don't feel or don't express.

Emails from my female students pour in about missing class because they are stuck at home with a sick baby and no childcare. Or crying after class about a bad grade, the result of a lack of time to study between work and mothering. I see my female students tackling more behind the scenes. Struggling to juggle more. Attempting to excel in more. And feeling deeply passionate about it all.

The biggest mistake I see my young female students make is in thinking they can't get everything they want out of life. They tend to stop themselves just short of going after it all. I see them settle for a mediocre relationship because they have a great job. Or become mothers and abandon their professional ambition. Give up on the idea of having kids because their future job will require so much travel.

When I was just starting off as a commuting adjunct, I was married but had no children. And it's clear to me now that my perception of women at that time was born out of my lack of knowledge about them. What I knew of women was that they were kinda mean in junior high, desperately trying to fit in during high school, fun as hell in college and competitive as coworkers. It was the gender to which I belonged. The gender of my best friend. My mother. My sister. But in many ways, I didn't necessarily feel a kinship.

So it wasn't just the powerful voices of the men or the fact that I was friends with boys that was driving my favoritism in the classroom. It was that my own relationship with women lacked depth and strength.

Luckily, that's what motherhood has given me. I instantly saw the differences in how my husband and I were treated as parents by outsiders. I saw the ways in which women struggled to achieve balance. Felt their selfishness conflict with their maternal instincts. Worked not to resent the men who didn't feel the same, or as much, pressure. Or to hate the women who seemed to be handling everything better. I had my own, often insurmountable, struggles with balance, body image, depression and discrimination. I've earned the ability to relate now to others.

While some women understood the need to support and love each other from a very young age, it really took the birth of my children for me to gain insight into the extremely dynamic and complicated role of being a woman. Any woman. Children or not. Married or not. Undergraduate or graduate. Team Tina or Team Amy.

Now, I spend many of my student interactions advising young women who are struggling to balance school and motherhood. Or trying to maintain a healthy marriage while coping with stress. Or worried about how having children will affect their careers. Or wondering what exactly to think about Lena Dunham.

So when I hear a knock on my office door, and turn around to see one of my bright female students standing there, I'm ready for her. If she's coming to me about a class assignment, I talk her through it. If she's coming to me for help selecting next semester's courses,

I give my feedback. But, if I'm lucky, she's there just to talk about life.

And if that's the case, I rely on the wisdom of my demanding, opinionated, negotiating three-year-old daughter at home—begging for a cookie to put on the kitchen table until after dinner—because she has taught me the most valuable lessons I've ever learned as a woman:

Ask for everything you want. Never take no for an answer. Find a way to have it all.

And leave nothing on the table.

Afterword:
Humbling Experience

I was walking down the hall of my high school when I saw, through the window of the freshman English class, Mrs. Humble standing at the podium.

Being a senior, and therefore understanding the rules no longer applied to me, I flung open the door and exclaimed, "Mrs. Humble!"

The class, startled, all turned toward me in their desks, and Mrs. Humble lifted her glasses from her chest, where they dangled on a chain, put them on and looked at me.

"Yes?" she said, with the same bird-like mannerisms I remembered from ten years earlier.

"It's me! Meg!" I practically yelled, still holding the door wide open. "I was in your third grade class!"

She stared at me for a bit.

It was possible she didn't remember me. It had been a decade since we last spoke.

"Of course, Meg!" she said, smiling and walking toward me.

We embraced at the door for a moment.

"What are you doing here?" I asked.

"Well," she said, her arm extended to the class I had rudely interrupted, "I'm substituting a little in my retirement."

"I'm so happy to see you again," I said.

"You too, Meg." And she walked back to the podium.

As I turned to leave, and just as the door was nearly closed, I heard her chime:

"And Meg?"

"Yes?" I said, opening the door again.

"I hope you are still writing."

After school that day, I asked my mother to give me back the book I had written in Mrs. Humble's third grade class. The one I vowed to never look at again.

My mom stared blankly at me.

Not only did she have no idea where the book was, she had no clue to what book I was referring.

Two important lessons came out of seeing Mrs. Humble that day:

One was that the most significant moments in a person's life are rarely equally significant to anyone else.

And the second was that, in the end, it didn't really matter if Mrs. Humble liked my book. Or hated my book. Or thought it was sloppy or derivative. It didn't even matter if she thought I was a bad writer. In the end, none of that mattered at all.

What mattered was that she supported me as a writer.

For that, I am eternally grateful to her.

And to you.

A Special Thanks

First and foremost, to my editor Jim Myers Morgan.
Sleeping with you really kept your fees low.

To the Morgan sisters, for all the material.
Living with you is the stuff of fiction.

To Liz Anderson, for designing the cover.
This book is lucky to be judged by it.

To my parents, for parenting.
And not in a showy way, like with a blog or a book.

To my siblings, for unknowingly convincing
me to have a second child.

To my best friend,
for a magical childhood.

To my students, for all you have taught me.
It really should have gone the other way.

To all the women in my life,
for making me proud of our gender.

To Tina Fey, for inspiring me in ways that are easier
to express in person. So please return my calls.

And finally, to Chasey Boom.
For making me believe in something
that seemed downright unimaginable.

For more of the same:
megmyersmorgan.com